Introduction to
Secure Outsourcing Computation

Synthesis Lectures on Information Security, Privacy, & Trust

Editors
Elisa Bertino, *Purdue University*
Ravi Sandhu, *University of Texas, San Antonio*

The *Synthesis Lectures Series on Information Security, Privacy, and Trust* publishes 50- to 100-page publications on topics pertaining to all aspects of the theory and practice of Information Security, Privacy, and Trust. The scope largely follows the purview of premier computer security research journals such as ACM Transactions on Information and System Security, IEEE Transactions on Dependable and Secure Computing and Journal of Cryptology, and premier research conferences, such as ACM CCS, ACM SACMAT, ACM AsiaCCS, ACM CODASPY, IEEE Security and Privacy, IEEE Computer Security Foundations, ACSAC, ESORICS, Crypto, EuroCrypt and AsiaCrypt. In addition to the research topics typically covered in such journals and conferences, the series also solicits lectures on legal, policy, social, business, and economic issues addressed to a technical audience of scientists and engineers. Lectures on significant industry developments by leading practitioners are also solicited.

Introduction to Secure Outsourcing Computation
Xiaofeng Chen
2016

Database Anonymization: Privacy Models, Data Utility, and Microaggregation-based
Inter-model Connections
Josep Domingo-Ferrer, David Sánchez, and Jordi Soria-Comas
2016

Automated Software Diversity
Per Larsen, Stefan Brunthaler, Lucas Davi, Ahmad-Reza Sadeghi, and Michael Franz
2015

Trust in Social Media
Jiliang Tang and Huan Liu
2015

Physically Unclonable Functions (PUFs): Applications, Models, and Future Directions
Christian Wachsmann and Ahmad-Reza Sadeghi
2014

Usable Security: History, Themes, and Challenges
Simson Garfinkel and Heather Richter Lipford
2014

Reversible Digital Watermarking: Theory and Practices
Ruchira Naskar and Rajat Subhra Chakraborty
2014

Mobile Platform Security
N. Asokan, Lucas Davi, Alexandra Dmitrienko, Stephan Heuser, Kari Kostiainen, Elena Reshetova, and Ahmad-Reza Sadeghi
2013

Security and Trust in Online Social Networks
Barbara Carminati, Elena Ferrari, and Marco Viviani
2013

RFID Security and Privacy
Yingjiu Li, Robert H. Deng, and Elisa Bertino
2013

Hardware Malware
Christian Krieg, Adrian Dabrowski, Heidelinde Hobel, Katharina Krombholz, and Edgar Weippl
2013

Private Information Retrieval
Xun Yi, Russell Paulet, and Elisa Bertino
2013

Privacy for Location-based Services
Gabriel Ghinita
2013

Enhancing Information Security and Privacy by Combining Biometrics with Cryptography
Sanjay G. Kanade, Dijana Petrovska-Delacrétaz, and Bernadette Dorizzi
2012

Analysis Techniques for Information Security
Anupam Datta, Somesh Jha, Ninghui Li, David Melski, and Thomas Reps
2010

Operating System Security
Trent Jaeger
2008

Introduction to Secure Outsourcing Computation

Xiaofeng Chen

ISBN: 978-3-031-01220-4 paperback
ISBN: 978-3-031-02348-4 ebook

DOI 10.1007/978-3-031-02348-4

A Publication in the Springer series
SYNTHESIS LECTURES ON INFORMATION SECURITY, PRIVACY, & TRUST

Lecture #16
Series Editors: Elisa Bertino, *Purdue University*
                Ravi Sandhu, *University of Texas, San Antonio*
Series ISSN
Print 1945-9742   Electronic 1945-9750

Introduction to
Secure Outsourcing Computation

Xiaofeng Chen
Xidian University, China

SYNTHESIS LECTURES ON INFORMATION SECURITY, PRIVACY, &
TRUST #16

ABSTRACT

With the rapid development of cloud computing, the enterprises and individuals can outsource their sensitive data into the cloud server where they can enjoy high quality data storage and computing services in a ubiquitous manner. This is known as the outsourcing computation paradigm. Recently, the problem for securely outsourcing various expensive computations or storage has attracted considerable attention in the academic community. In this book, we focus on the latest technologies and applications of secure outsourcing computations. Specially, we introduce the state-of-the-art research for secure outsourcing some specific functions such as scientific computations, cryptographic basic operations, and verifiable large database with update. The constructions for specific functions use various design tricks and thus result in very efficient protocols for real-world applications.

The topic of outsourcing computation is a hot research issue nowadays. Thus, this book will be beneficial to academic researchers in the field of cloud computing and big data security.

KEYWORDS

cloud computing, verifiable computing, outsourcing paradigm, privacy preserving, security model

Dedicated to my precious wife and lovely daughter

Contents

Preface xi

Acknowledgments xiii

1 Introduction 1

    1.1 Outsourcing Paradigm in Cloud Computing 2

    1.2 Secure Challenges in Outsourcing Computation 3

    1.3 Formal Security Definition 4

        1.3.1 Security Requirements 5

        1.3.2 Adversarial Model 6

    1.4 General Construction 8

2 Preliminaries 11

    2.1 Number-Theoretic Problems 11

    2.2 Bilinear Pairings (Groups of Prime Order) 11

    2.3 Bilinear Pairings (Groups of Composite Order) 12

    2.4 Sparse Matrix and Dense Matrix 13

    2.5 Vector Commitments 14

    2.6 Algebraic Pseudorandom Functions 15

    2.7 Bloom Filter 17

3 Secure Outsourcing of Scientific Computations 19

    3.1 Matrix Multiplication 19

        3.1.1 A Basic Solution 20

        3.1.2 An Enhanced Solution 21

    3.2 Matrix Inversion 22

    3.3 Large-scale Linear Equations Systems 23

        3.3.1 New Secure Outsourcing Protocol 24

        3.3.2 Security Analysis 26

4   **Secure Outsourcing of Cryptographic Operations** **29**

    4.1   Security Definitions 30

    4.2   Two Untrusted Program Model 33

    4.3   Secure Outsourcing of Single Modular Exponentiation 33

        4.3.1   The Proposed Algorithm 35

        4.3.2   Security Analysis 36

        4.3.3   Comparison 38

    4.4   Secure Outsourcing of Simultaneous Modular Exponentiation 38

        4.4.1   Outsourcing Algorithm 39

        4.4.2   Efficiency 40

    4.5   Secure Outsourcing of Bilinear Pairings 40

        4.5.1   Outsourcing Algorithm 41

        4.5.2   Improved Outsourcing Algorithm 42

5   **Secure Outsourcing of Large Database With Updates** **45**

    5.1   Security Definitions 46

        5.1.1   Security Requirements 47

        5.1.2   Forward Automatic/Backward Substitution Update Attack 48

    5.2   VDB Construction From Delegating Polynomial Functions 49

        5.2.1   Delegating of Polynomial Functions 49

        5.2.2   Benabbas-Gennaro-Vahlis VDB Construction 50

    5.3   VDB Framework Based on Vector Commitment 51

        5.3.1   The General Framework 51

        5.3.2   Security Analysis 52

    5.4   VDB Framework From Binding Vector Commitment 54

        5.4.1   A Concrete VDB Scheme 56

        5.4.2   Security Analysis of the VDB Scheme 57

    5.5   Incremental VDB Framework 58

        5.5.1   Incremental Encryption Based on Bit Flipping 59

        5.5.2   Inc-VDB Framework 61

        5.5.3   A Concrete Inc-VDB Scheme 62

6   **Conclusion and Future Works** **65**

    Bibliography **67**

    Author's Biography **79**

Preface

Cloud computing, the new term for the long dreamed vision of computing as a utility, offers plenty of benefits for real-world applications, such as on-demand self-service, ubiquitous network access, location independent resource pooling, rapid resource elasticity, usage-based pricing, outsourcing, etc. The most outstanding benefit of cloud computing is the so-called outsourcing paradigm. That is, the users with resource-constraint devices can outsource heavy computation workloads into the cloud server and enjoy the unlimited computing resources in a pay-per-use manner. As a result, the enterprises and individuals can avoid large capital outlays in hardware/software deployment and maintenance. Despite these benefits, the outsourcing paradigm also inevitably suffers from some new security challenges due to untrusted cloud servers. Thus, how to securely outsource prohibitively expensive computations is a hot issue in academic research community.

The general construction for securely outsourcing arbitrary functions has been proposed based on the primitives of garbled circuit and full homomorphic encryption. In this sense, the problem of secure outsourcing computation has been theoretically solved. However, this general solution is inefficient for most real applications and thus it is meaningful to seek efficient outsourcing protocols for various specific functions. This book addresses the advances of secure outsourcing computations. More specifically, we focus on the state-of-the-art techniques of secure outsourcing computations for different specific functions based on different design tricks. In Chapter 1, we give a brief introduction for secure outsourcing computation, including its security challenges and formal security definitions. In Chapter 2, we present some preliminaries which will be used in this book. Chapter 3 presents in detail some recent research for securely outsourcing scientific computations. In Chapter 4, we present some recent techniques for securely outsourcing cryptographic operations, such as modular exponentiations and bilinear parings. Recent progress in verifiable outsourcing very large databases with efficient updates is presented in Chapter 5. Finally, we conclude and discuss future research directions in Chapter 6.

Xiaofeng Chen
February 2016

Acknowledgments

Parts of the content of this lecture are results of research projects funded by the National Natural Science Foundation of China (No. 61572382) and Program for New Century Excellent Talents in University (No. NCET-13-0946).

I sincerely express my gratitude to Prof. Attila Yavuz at Oregon State University and Prof. Fang-Yu Rao at Purdue University for their invaluable suggestions to improve this book. I would also like to thank my three Ph.D. students, Jianfeng Wang, Hui Huang, and Zhiwei Zhang, for their help when the book was being written.

Xiaofeng Chen
February 2016

CHAPTER 1

Introduction

In this chapter, we present the security challenges and formal definitions of secure outsourcing computation. We also introduce the general outsourcing framework of an arbitrary function introduced by Gennaro, Gentry, and Parno [74].

Let us consider some scenarios in the real applications. For example, if you want to travel the world by air, would you like the idea of buying a very expensive Boeing 737? I guess that the overwhelming majority of people would not because the plane is too expensive. Of course, it is another thing if you are Jackie Chan. Fortunately, most of us need not buy a Boeing 737, but a flight ticket for traveling. In this example, we can outsource a very expensive task to a service provider (e.g., an airline company) and just enjoy the service in a pay-per-use manner.

Nowadays, we always encounter some prohibitively expensive computation tasks. For example, the sieving for factoring a 768-bit RSA modulus took almost two years on many hundreds of machines. However, on a single core 2.2 GHz AMD Opteron processor with 2 GB RAM, performing this algorithm would have taken about 1,500 years [89]. Trivially, in order to accomplish this kind of computation task, the resource-limited client has no choice but to outsource it to servers with rich resources.

In some cases, even if we can afford certain expensive tasks, they are not worthy it. For example, would you like to buy a $10,000 wedding dress that you will wear only once in your life? From the viewpoint of a rational economic person, the right thing is to rent it from a wedding dress store. That is, we could outsource this kind of expensive task to a service provider.

From the above examples, we could have an informal definition for outsourcing computation. That is, the clients with resource-constraint devices delegate the heavy computation workloads into the powerful servers and pay for the services. Trivially, outsourcing computation can offer significant benefits to IT enterprises, especially in the period of financial crisis, since large capital outlays on hardware/software deployment and maintenance are avoided. However, we argue that outsourcing computation is not a panacea to solve all problems in the environment of limited resources. The reason is that we should not only consider the computational resources in the outsourcing paradigm, but also other types of resources, such as storage, communication (bandwidth), and energy (electric power). Recently, Chen and Sion [59] explored the relationship between the costs and security aspects in cloud computing, and pointed out that secure outsourcing computation is only meaningful in some special scenarios. Indeed, there are always hidden costs of bandwidth, which are costlier than computation itself, as well as energy consumption. Therefore, we must carefully evaluate the tool of outsourcing computation and utilize it correctly.

Throughout this book, we only consider the "challenge-response" type of outsourcing protocols. That is, the client sends the computation task and then the server responds with the result. These kinds of protocols require only one round of interaction between the client and the server. We argue that the protocols with multiple rounds of interaction are impractical in real applications.

1.1   OUTSOURCING PARADIGM IN CLOUD COMPUTING

Cloud computing, the new term for the long dreamed vision of computing as a utility, enables ubiquitous, convenient, and on-demand network access to a centralized pool of configurable computing resources [110]. Cloud computing offers many benefits, such as fast deployment, pay-per-use, low-costs, rapid elasticity, ubiquitous network access, etc. One of the fundamental advantages of cloud computing is the so-called outsourcing paradigm, where the clients with resource-constraint devices can outsource the heavy computation workloads into untrusted cloud servers and enjoy the unlimited computing resources in a pay-per-use manner. That is, the computation resources are now viewed as an infrastructure and platform to provide for the paying clients as a service.

Generally, we can view any computation task as a function $F : D \to M$ on a domain D such that $F(D) \subseteq M$. Given any $x \in D$, the goal is to compute $F(x)$. In the outsourcing paradigm, an honest but resources-contained client C wants to delegate the computation task $F(x)$ to a cloud server S that is not fully trusted by C. Firstly, C may outsource the encoding of F and x to C (that is, the information about F and x should be kept secret to S in some scenarios). Secondly, C returns the computation result based on the input (note that the output is not $F(x)$). The client Finally, C efficiently verifies that the output provided by S is valid and then computes the final result $F(x)$ by himself. The outsourcing paradigm in cloud computing is illustrated in Fig. 1.1 (note that we have implicitly presented three security requirements of outsourcing computation which will be given in more detail below).

Secure outsourcing computation is also termed as verifiable computation or delegation of computation. Secure outsourcing computation is closely related to the primitive of secure multiparty computation (MPC), in which a set of players $P_1, P_2, \ldots, P_n$ securely compute a given function F on the inputs $x_1, x_2, \ldots, x_n$ [38]. Define $F(x_1, x_2, \ldots, x_n) = (y_1, y_2, \ldots, y_n)$. The security in MPC means that each player P_i can only learn the information of y_i. This is very similar to the input/output secrecy of outsourcing computation. The main difference between the two notations is that the computational resources of each player in MPC is assumed to be (almost) the same. While in the outsourcing computation paradigm, the client is assumed to have insufficient resources to accomplish the computation of F. Besides, each party in MPC aims to obtain a corresponding computation result. However, in the outsourcing computation, only the client really cares about the computation result. Even if some server is also curious about the result, this is not the part of the protocol. Finally, in the outsourcing computation, the computation

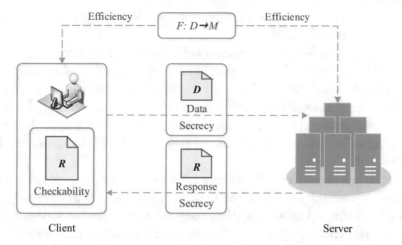

Figure 1.1: Secure outsourcing paradigm in cloud computing.

is viewed as a service and the client must pay the server for the service. While in MPC, no party will be paid by others.

1.2   SECURE CHALLENGES IN OUTSOURCING COMPUTATION

With the availability of cloud services, the techniques for securely outsourcing the expensive computaions to untrusted cloud servers are getting more and more attention in the scientific community [1, 7, 13, 45, 49, 50, 92]. However, on the other hand, the outsourcing paradigm also inevitably introduces some new security concerns and challenges [111, 125]. Basically, there are three security challenges as shown below.

Firstly, the cloud servers can only be assumed to be semi-trusted, while the computation tasks often contain some sensitive information that should not be exposed to the cloud servers. Thus, the first security challenge is the *secrecy* of the outsourcing computation: the cloud servers should not learn anything about what it is actually computing (including the *secret* inputs and the outputs). We argue that the encryption can only provide a partial solution to this problem since it is very difficult to perform meaningful computations over the encrypted data. Note that fully homomorphic encryption could be a potential solution to this problem, but the existing schemes are not practical yet for real-world applications.

Secondly, the semi-trusted cloud servers may return some invalid results. For example, the servers might contain a software bug that will fail on a constant number of invocations. Moreover, the servers might decrease the amount of the computations due to financial incentives and then return computationally indistinguishable (invalid) results. Therefore, the second security challenge is the *checkability* of the outsourcing computation: the client should have the ability to detect any failures if the cloud servers misbehave.

Finally, the last challenge is the *efficiency* of the outsourcing computation. That is, the verification algorithm is very efficient and should never require some other complicated computations. Otherwise, the outourcing will become meaningless. At least, the (computation and storage) overload of the client must be much less than that for accomplishing the computation task itself. Besides, the communication overload should also be considered as a factor of efficiency in outsourcing protocols. That is, the outsourcing protocols should not require multiple rounds of interactions between the client and servers.

In general, we can achieve the secrecy by means of special encryption or disguise (also known as blinding) techniques. Thus, the remaining issue is how to efficiently verify the computation results. Without loss of generality, there are three kinds of approaches to achieve the verifiability of outsourcing computations. The first one is mostly suitable for the case that the verification itself is not involved in any expensive computations. For example, for the "inversion of one-way function" class of outsourcing computations [22, 45, 61, 62, 79], the client can directly verify the result since the verification is just equivalent to compute the one-way functions. The second approach is that the client uses multiple servers to achieve verifiability [45, 58, 82]. That is, the client sends the random test query to multiple servers and it accepts only if all the servers output the same result. Trivially, the approach can only ensure the client to detect the error with probability absolutely less than 1. The last approach is based on one malicious server and might leverage some proof systems [73, 87, 88, 96]. Obviously, an essential requirement is that the client must verify the proofs efficiently.

1.3   FORMAL SECURITY DEFINITION

Gennaro, Gentry, and Parno [74] presented a formal definition for securely outsourcing computation, which consists of the following algorithms:

- **KeyGen** $(\mathsf{F}, \lambda) \rightarrow (PK, SK)$: The randomized key generation algorithm generates a public key PK that encodes the target function F with the security parameter λ, which is used by the server to compute F. Then a corresponding secret key SK is generated and kept private by the client.

- **ProbGen** $_{SK}(x) \rightarrow (\sigma_x, \tau_x)$: The problem generation algorithm uses the secret key SK to encode the function input x as a public value σ_x which is given to the server to compute with, and a secret value τ_x is kept private by the client.

- **Compute** $_{PK}(\sigma_x) \rightarrow \sigma_y$: Using the public key PK and the encoded input σ_x, the server computes an encoded version σ_y of the output $y = \mathsf{F}(x)$.

- **Verify** $_{SK}(\tau_x, \sigma_y) \to y \cup \bot$: Using the client's secret key SK and the secret "decoding" τ_x, the verification algorithm converts the server's encoded output σ_y into the output of the function, e.g., $y = \mathsf{F}(x)$, or outputs $\bot$ if σ_y is invalid.

Trivially, a secure outsourcing computation scheme should be correct. That is, the computation result σ_y by an honest server will always be successfully verified and the algorithm **Verify** outputs y. In this sense, we say that C^S correctly implements the function F.

1.3.1   SECURITY REQUIREMENTS

In the following, we introduce some security requirements for outsourcing computation [74, 82].

The first requirement is the *privacy* for the input/output of the computation task. Informally, it means that the server cannot learn anything from its interaction in the protocol in the sense of an indistinguishability argument.

Definition 1.1   (privacy) Given a security parameter k, a pair of algorithms (C, S) achieves the privacy for the input/output of F if for any probabilistic polynomial time (PPT) adversary A,

$$\mathrm{Adv}_A^{C^S}(\mathsf{F}, k) \leq \mathrm{negl}(k),$$

where $\mathrm{Adv}_A^{C^S}(\mathsf{F}, k) = |\Pr[b = b'] - \frac{1}{2}|$ is defined as the advantage of A in the experiment as follows:

$$
\begin{aligned}
&(PK, SK) \overset{R}{\leftarrow} \mathbf{KeyGen}(\mathsf{F}, k); \\
&(x_0, x_1) \leftarrow A^{\mathbf{PubProbGen}_{SK}(\cdot)}(PK) \\
&(\sigma_0, \tau_0) \leftarrow \mathbf{ProbGen}_{SK}(x_0); \\
&(\sigma_1, \tau_1) \leftarrow \mathbf{ProbGen}_{SK}(x_1); \\
&b \overset{R}{\leftarrow} \{0, 1\}; \\
&b' \leftarrow A^{\mathbf{PubProbGen}_{SK}(\cdot)}(PK, x_0, x_1, \sigma_b).
\end{aligned}
$$

During the above experiment, the adversary A is allowed to request the encoding of any input he desires. The oracle **PubProbGen**$_{SK}(x)$ calls **ProbGen**$_{SK}(x)$ to obtain (σ_x, τ_x) and returns only the public part σ_x. Trivially, the output of **PubProbGen**$_{SK}(x)$ is probabilistic.

The second requirement is the *efficiency* of outsourcing algorithms. That is, the local computation done by client C should be substantially less than that to accomplish the original computation by itself (i.e., without outsourcing). Note that the local computation consists of the computational overload of algorithms **ProbGen** and **Verify**. However, it does not include the computation of **KeyGen** which may be prohibitively heavy since it can be amortized over plenty of different input computations.

Definition 1.2   (α-**efficiency**) A pair of algorithms (C, S) is said to be an α-efficient implementation of F if (1) C^S correctly implements F and (2) for $\forall\ x \in D$, the running time of C is no more than an α-multiplicative factor of the running time of F, where $0 < \alpha < 1$.

The last requirement is the *checkability* (also known as verifiability) of outsourcing algorithms. That is, the output by the server must be *checked* for correctness. More precisely, the invalid output given by any malicious server cannot pass the verification and client C will detect the error with a non-negligible probability.

Definition 1.3   (**checkability**) Given a security parameter k, a pair of algorithms (C, S) achieve the checkability for F if for any probabilistic polynomial time (PPT) adversary A,

$$\mathrm{Adv}_A^{CS}(\mathsf{F}, k) \leq \mathrm{negl}(k),$$

where $\mathrm{Adv}_A^{CS}(\mathsf{F}, k) = \Pr[\mathbf{Exp}(\mathsf{F}, k) = 1]$ is defined as the advantage of A in the experiment **Exp** as follows:

$$
\begin{aligned}
&(PK, SK) \overset{R}{\leftarrow} \mathbf{KeyGen}(\mathsf{F}, k); \\
&\text{For } i = 1, 2, \ldots, l = poly(k); \\
&\qquad x_i \leftarrow A(PK, x_1, \sigma_1, \ldots, x_{i-1}, \sigma_{i-1}) \\
&\qquad (\sigma_i, \tau_i) \leftarrow \mathbf{ProbGen}_{SK}(x_i); \\
&(i, \hat{\sigma}_y) \leftarrow A(PK, x_1, \sigma_1, \ldots, x_l, \sigma_l); \\
&\hat{y} \leftarrow \mathbf{Verify}_{SK}(\tau_i, \hat{\sigma}_y) \\
&\text{If } \hat{y} \neq \perp \wedge \hat{y} \neq \mathsf{F}(x_i), \text{output } '1'; \text{else } '0';
\end{aligned}
$$

Also, we can define the magnitude of checkability in a secure outsourcing scheme. That is, a pair of algorithms (C, S) is said to be a β-checkable implementation of F if (1) C^S correctly implements F and (2) for $\forall\ x \in D$, if a malicious S' deviates from its advertised functionality during the execution of $C^{S'}(x)$, C will detect the error with probability no less than $0 < \beta \leq 1$.

1.3.2 ADVERSARIAL MODEL

In this section, we introduce four kinds of adversarial models for secure outsourcing computation. Note that the adversary is the untrusted server(s) in all models.

- **Honest-but-curious Model**

   The "honest-but-curious model" (also-called the semi-honest model) was firstly introduced by Goldreich et al. [78]. In this model, both the client C and the server S are guaranteed to properly execute a prescribed protocol, but, at the end of it, S can use its own view of the execution to infer about C's input. Therefore, S will honestly send the computation results to C. But he will try his best to retrieve some sensitive information such as the secret input/output of C. Note that the computation results (i.e., the output of S) are different from the output of C (i.e., the real computation aim of C).

- **Lazy-but-honest Model**

  The "Lazy-but-honest model" was first introduced by Golle and Mironov [79], which is suitable for the inversion of the one-way function class of outsourcing computations. Similarly, in this model, S will also honestly send the computation results to C if and only if he has accomplished the computation. However, S is viewed as a rational economic person and will try to minimize the amount of computation overload in order to save the computational resources. In the worst case, S will send a computational indistinguishable or even random result to C. As a result, C should be able to verify the result efficiently.

- **Two Untrusted Program Model**

  Hohenberger and Lysyanskaya [82] first introduced the "two untrusted program model" for outsourcing cryptographic computations. The two untrusted program model, in brief, is the model that there are two non-colluding servers S_1 and S_2, and we assume at most one of them is adversarial while we cannot know which one. Besides, the misbehavior of the dishonest server can be detected with an overwhelming probability. This model is suitable for designing the secure outsourcing scheme for the expensive operations in a cryptographic algorithm such as modular exponentiation or bilinear pair.

- **Refereed Delegation of Computation Model**

  The "refereed delegation of computation model" was first introduced by Canetti et al. [58], where the client C delegates the computation to $n \geq 2$ servers $S_1, S_2, \ldots S_n$ under the assumption that at least one of the servers is honest. In case the servers make contradictory claims about the computation results, C can engage in a protocol with each of the servers, at the end of which C can efficiently determine the true claim under the assumption that at least one of the servers is honest (while the client does not know which is honest). Obviously, the two untrusted program model can be viewed as a special case of refereed delegation of computation model when the number of servers $n = 2$.

- **Amortized Model**

  Gennaro, Gentry, and Parno [74] firstly introduce the "amortized model" to construct efficient verifiable computation protocols. By introducing an expensive pre-processing stage, the client C can outsource some computation-intensive tasks to the server S in an efficient manner. Although C needs to perform a one-time complicated computation in the pre-processing stage, the computation overload is amortized over all future executions. Note that the pre-processing is performed only once, C could outsource it to a trusted server or perform it in an offline manner.

1.4   GENERAL CONSTRUCTION

In 2010, Gennaro, Gentry, and Parno [74] first formalized the definition for secure outsourcing computation (they called it the notion of verifiable computation) and presented a milstone theoretic framework for secure outsourcing arbitrary computation functions as shown in Fig. 1.2. The framework mainly uses two building blocks of garbled circuit [130, 131] and fully homomorphic encryption [69, 70, 118, 124].

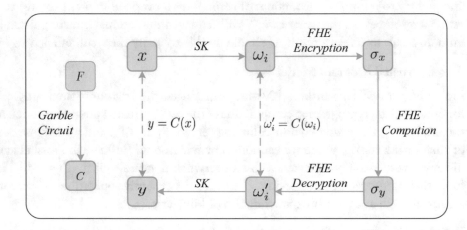

Figure 1.2: General construction.

In this section, we give a brief introduction to Gennaro et al.'s general outsourcing framework. The main idea is as follows: Our task is to compute $y = F(x)$. Firstly, the client converts the target function F as a garbled circuit C using Yao's protocol. The client keeps all the wire values $\{w_i\}$ as his private key SK and the ciphertexts $\{\gamma_i\}$ on each gate g as his public key PK. Now, there is a one-to-one correspondence between some wire values w_i and the binary expression of x. Note that w_i is the secret key and could not exposed to the servers. Thus, the client should encrypt w_i and this is accomplished by using a fully homomorphic encryption scheme FHE with the public/secret key pair (PK_E, SK_E). As we know, there are two encryption operations in FHE. The client performs the first operation and encrypts w_i with the public key PK_E and sends the ciphertext σ_x to the server. On the other hand, the client outsources the second (expensive) operation **Evaluate** to the server and let the ciphertext be σ_y. Due to the property of fully homomorphic encryption, we know that σ_y should be the ciphertext of ω_i', where ω_i' is the wire values representing $y = C(x) = F(x)$ in binary. Trivially, the client can decrypt σ_y with

SK_E and obtain ω_i'. Finally, the client uses the private key SK to map ω_i' to the computation result y.

The general construction consists of the following algorithms:

- **KeyGen**$(F, \lambda) \rightarrow (PK, SK)$: Represent F as a garbled circuit C using Yao's circuit construction. Choose two random values $\omega_i^0, \omega_i^1 \leftarrow \{0, 1\}^\lambda$ for each wire ω_i. For each gate g, compute the four ciphertexts $(\gamma_{00}^g, \gamma_{01}^g, \gamma_{10}^g, \gamma_{11}^g)$. The public key $PK \leftarrow \cup_g (\gamma_{00}^g, \gamma_{01}^g, \gamma_{10}^g, \gamma_{11}^g)$, and the secret key $SK \leftarrow \cup_i (\omega_i^0, \omega_i^1)$.

- **ProbGen**$_{SK}(x) \rightarrow \sigma_x$: Run the key generation algorithm of a fully homomorphic encryption scheme to create a new key pair $(PK_E, SK_E) \leftarrow \textbf{KeyGen}_E(\lambda)$. Let $\omega_x \subset SK$ be the wire values representing the binary expression of x. Set the public value $\sigma_x \leftarrow \textbf{Enc}_E(PK_E, \omega_x)$ and the private value $\tau_x \leftarrow SK_E$.

- **Compute**$_{PK}(\sigma_x) \rightarrow \sigma_y$: Construct a circuit Δ that on input ω, ω', γ outputs $D_\omega(D_{\omega'}(\gamma))$, where D is the decryption algorithm corresponding to the encryption E used in Yao's garbling (therefore Δ computes the appropriate decryption in Yao's construction). Calculate $\textbf{Evaluate}_E(\Delta, \textbf{Enc}_E(PK_E, \omega_x), \textbf{Enc}_E(PK_E, \gamma_i))$ repeatedly, to decrypt your way through the ciphertexts, just as in the evaluation of Yao's garbled circuit. The result is $\sigma_y \leftarrow \textbf{Enc}_E(PK_E, \omega_i')$, where ω_i' is the wire values representing $y = F(x)$ in binary.

- **Verify**$_{SK}(\sigma_y) \rightarrow y \cup \bot$: Decrypt σ_y with SK_E to obtain ω_i'. Use SK to map the wire values to an output y. If the decryption or mapping fails, then output $\bot$.

Though the above solution allows a client to outsource the computation of an arbitrary function, it is inefficient for practical applications due to the complicated fully homomorphic encryption techniques. Besides, another disadvantage of the schemes based on fully homomorphic encryption is that the client must repeat the expensive pre-processing stage if the malicious server tries to cheat and learns a bit of information, i.e., the client has accepted or rejected the computation result. In this sense, even the problem of outsourcing computation has been theoretically solved, it is still meaningful to seek secure and efficient outsourcing computation protocols for specific functions.

In the remainder of this book, we mainly focus on the concrete constructions of secure outsourcing computation for specific functions using various design tricks.

CHAPTER 2

Preliminaries

In this chapter, we introduce some preliminaries for this book. We assume that the readers have some basic knowledge of number theory, basic algebra, and cryptography and thus will not present them here.

2.1 NUMBER-THEORETIC PROBLEMS

Let $\mathbb{G}$ be a cyclic multiplicative group of prime order p, and g is a generator of $\mathbb{G}$. We introduce some intractable problems in $\mathbb{G}$, and intractability means that by far there is no polynomial time algorithm to solve these problems with non-negligible probability.

- Discrete Logarithm Problem (DLP): Given two elements (g, h) as inputs, to find an integer $x \in \mathbb{Z}_p^*$ such that $h = g^x$ whenever such an integer exists. We say that the DL assumption holds in $\mathbb{G}$ if for every probabilistic polynomial time algorithm $\mathcal{A}$, there exists a negligible function $negl(\cdot)$ such that $\Pr[\mathcal{A}(1^k, g, h) = x] \leq negl(k)$ for all security parameter k.

- Computational Diffie-Hellman Problem (CDHP): Given a triple (g, g^x, g^y) for any $x, y \in_R \mathbb{Z}_p$ as inputs, output g^{xy}.

- Square Computational Diffie-Hellman Problem (Squ-CDHP): Given (g, g^x) for $x \in_R \mathbb{Z}_p$ as inputs, output g^{x^2}. It has been proved that the Squ-CDH assumption is equivalent to the classical CDH assumption [10].

- Decisional Diffie-Hellman Problem (DDHP): Given a triple (g, g^x, g^y, g^z) for any $x, y, z \in_R \mathbb{Z}_p$ as inputs, to decide whether $z \equiv xy \mod p$.

- Strong Diffie-Hellman Problem (SDHP): Given a tuple $(g, g^x, g^{x^2}, \cdots, g^{x^l})$ for any $x \in_R \mathbb{Z}_p$ as inputs, output a pair $(c, g^{\frac{1}{x+c}})$.

- Strong Decisional Diffie-Hellman Problem (SDDHP): Given two tuples $(g, g^x, g^{x^2}, \cdots, g^{x^l})$ and $(g, g^{x_1}, g^{x_2}, \cdots, g^{x_l})$ for any $x, x_1, \cdots, x_l \in_R \mathbb{Z}_p$ as inputs, to decide which is the random tuple.

2.2 BILINEAR PAIRINGS (GROUPS OF PRIME ORDER)

Let $\mathbb{G}_1$, $\mathbb{G}_2$, and $\mathbb{G}_T$ be three cyclic multiplicative groups of prime order p. Let g_1 and g_2 be a generator of $\mathbb{G}_1$ and $\mathbb{G}_2$, respectively. Define an isomorphism $\psi : \mathbb{G}_2 \to \mathbb{G}_1$ with $\psi(g_2) = g_1$ and its inverse $\psi^{-1} : \mathbb{G}_1 \to \mathbb{G}_2$. A bilinear pairing is a map $e : \mathbb{G}_1 \times \mathbb{G}_2 \to \mathbb{G}_T$ with the following properties:

1. Bilinear: $e(u^a, v^b) = e(u, v)^{ab}$ for all $u \in \mathbb{G}_1$, $v \in \mathbb{G}_2$, and $a, b \in \mathbb{Z}_p^*$.

2. Non-degenerate: $e(g_1, g_2) \neq 1$.

3. Computable: There is an efficient algorithm to compute $e(u, v)$ for all $u \in \mathbb{G}_1$, $v \in \mathbb{G}_2$.

The examples of such groups can be found in certain algebraic varieties or curves over finite fields, and the bilinear pairings can be derived from the Weil or Tate pairings and some variants thereof. For more details, see [11, 27, 36, 81]. It has been proved that the CDHP and DDHP are not equivalent in the group $\mathbb{G}_1$ and thus called a gap Diffie-Hellman (GDH) group. More precisely, we call $\mathbb{G}_1$ a GDH group if the DDHP can be solved in polynomial time but there is no polynomial time algorithm to solve the CDHP with non-negligible probability.

Using the terminology of [81], we can separate the bilinear pairings into the following three types.

• Type 1: $\mathbb{G}_1 = \mathbb{G}_2$ or, both ψ and ψ^{-1} are efficiently computable.

• Type 2: $\mathbb{G}_1 \neq \mathbb{G}_2$ and, either ψ or ψ^{-1} is efficiently computable but not both.

• Type 3: $\mathbb{G}_1 \neq \mathbb{G}_2$ and, neither ψ nor ψ^{-1} is efficiently computable.

Note that $\mathbb{G}_1$ and $\mathbb{G}_2$ are cyclic groups of the same order, thus ψ, ψ^{-1} certainly exist. Also, as argued in [81], "not efficiently computable" does not necessarily mean "infeasible to compute."

2.3   BILINEAR PAIRINGS (GROUPS OF COMPOSITE ORDER)

Generally, we often use bilinear pairings on groups of prime order. Recently, pairings on groups of composite order have been used to design new cryptographic schemes such as non-interactive zero-knowledge proofs [75, 76], attribute-based encryption [32, 91], and database with efficient update [18].

The primitive of bilinear pairings over composite order groups was first introduced by Boneh, Goh, and Nissim [17]. The definition for bilinear groups with composite order is almost the same as that with prime order. The only difference is that the order of the groups are a composite $n = pq$ where the factorization of n is kept secret. As remarked in [81], it seems that the academic community generally uses the Type 1 setting for bilinear groups of composite order.

Let $\mathbb{G}_1$ and $\mathbb{G}_T$ be two cyclic multiplicative groups of composite order $n = pq$. A bilinear pairing is a map $e : \mathbb{G}_1 \times \mathbb{G}_1 \to \mathbb{G}_T$ that satisfies the properties of bilinear, non-degenerate, and computable. Bilinear groups of composite order are pairs of groups $(\mathbb{G}_1, \mathbb{G}_T)$ that are equipped with the map e. In the following, we introduce the subgroup decision problem in $(\mathbb{G}_1, \mathbb{G}_T)$.

- Subgroup Decision Problem: Let $n = pq$ where p, q are two large primes. Let $(\mathbb{G}_1, \mathbb{G}_T, e)$ be bilinear groups of order n. Given an element $x \in \mathbb{G}_1$, output '1' if the order of x is p and output '0' otherwise; that is, without knowing the factorization of n, decide if an element $x \in \mathbb{G}_1$ is in a subgroup of $\mathbb{G}_1$. We say that the subgroup decision assumption holds if for every PPT distinguisher $\mathcal{A}$ there exists a negligible function neg(.) such that for all λ,

$$|\Pr[\mathcal{A}(n, \mathbb{G}_1, \mathbb{G}_T, e, x) = 1] - \Pr[\mathcal{A}(n, \mathbb{G}_1, \mathbb{G}_T, e, x^q) = 1]| \leq neg(\lambda)$$

Informally, the assumption indicates that the uniform distribution on $\mathbb{G}_1$ is indistinguishable from the uniform distribution on a subgroup of $\mathbb{G}_1$.

There is an interesting property for pairings over composite order groups: Let $\mathbb{G}_p$ and $\mathbb{G}_q$ be subgroups of $\mathbb{G}_1$ of orders p and q, respectively. For any $u \in \mathbb{G}_p$ and $v \in \mathbb{G}_q$, we have $e(u, v) = 1_{\mathbb{G}_T}$. Note that this property holds for every pairing over composite order groups. The reason is as follows:

Let g be a generator of $\mathbb{G}_1$. Then g^p generates $\mathbb{G}_q$ and g^q generates $\mathbb{G}_p$. So there exist some a, b that satisfy $u = (g^q)^a$ and $v = (g^p)^b$. Then we can deduce that

$$e(u, v) = e(g^{aq}, g^{bp}) = e(g^a, g^b)^n = 1_{\mathbb{G}_T}.$$

For the practical application, note that the size of n should be at least 1,024 bits. Besides, in order to achieve the equivalent level of security, the size of a prime-order bilinear groups is only about 160 bits. Thus, the operations in composite-order bilinear groups are much slower than that in prime-order bilinear groups. This illustrates why the prime-order bilinear groups are the optimal choice for pairing-based schemes unless they fail to work.

2.4   SPARSE MATRIX AND DENSE MATRIX

The word "matrix" means something that contains the essence of a thing [85]. In linear algebra, a matrix is a rectangular array of numbers, symbols, or expressions, arranged in rows and columns. The individual items in a matrix are called its elements or entries.

A major application of matrices is to solve the solution of systems of linear equations. The reason is that matrices can be used to compactly represent systems of linear equations. For example, let $A = (a_{ij})$ be an $m \times n$ matrix, x'' be a column vector (i.e., $n \times 1$ matrix) of n variables $x_1, x_2, \cdots, x_n$, and b'' be an $m \times 1$ column vector, then the matrix equation $Ax'' = b''$ is equivalent to the system of linear equations:

$$\begin{cases} a_{1,1}x_1 + a_{1,2}x_2 + \cdots + a_{1,n}x_n = b_1 \\ a_{2,1}x_1 + a_{2,2}x_2 + \cdots + a_{2,n}x_n = b_2 \\ \qquad\qquad \vdots \qquad\qquad \vdots \\ a_{m,1}x_1 + a_{m,2}x_2 + \cdots + a_{m,n}x_n = b_m \end{cases} \tag{2.1}$$

In many real-world applications, some additional information about the matrices is known beforehand. For example, the predominant entries of a matrix are zero. This kind of matrix is called sparse matrix. By contrast, if most of the entries of a matrix are non-zero, then the matrix is dense. The fraction of zero entries over the total number of elements in a matrix is called the sparsity. Large-scale sparse matrices play an important role in solving partial differential equations in scientific or engineering applications. Besides, when A is sparse, it is easier and faster to solve the systems of linear equations $Ax'' = b''$.

We list some facts for sparse matrices without proof. Interested readers could give a proof. In the following, we assume that both M and N are two large $n \times n$ square matrices.

- If both M and N are dense, it is well known that the computational complexity of MN is $O(n^3)$. While if M is sparse and N is dense, the computational complexity is only $O(n^2)$.

- Even if both M and N are sparse, we could not know the sparsity of MN. Actually, MN may be sparse or extremely dense!

- If M is a sparse matrix, then M may be singular or non-singular (i.e., invertible).

- If M is a sparse matrix, then the inverse matrix M^{-1} (if it exists) may be extremely dense. That is, the computational complexity of M^{-1} is $O(n^3)$ in some cases. Thus, it is not wise to solve linear equations with M^{-1}. Actually, we should never solve linear equations with the inverse matrix.

- Both iterative and direct methods can be used to solve systems of linear equations whether the matrix is sparse or not.

2.5   VECTOR COMMITMENTS

Commitment is a fundamental primitive in cryptography and plays an important role in almost all security protocols, such as voting, identification zero-knowledge proof, etc. Intuitively, a commitment scheme can be viewed as the digital equivalent of a sealed envelope. In the commitment stage, the sender places a message in the sealed envelope and gives it to the receiver. In the opening stage, the sender reveals the message to the receiver. On the one hand, no one except the sender could open the envelope to learn the message from the commitment (this is called hiding). On the other hand, the sender could not change the message anymore (this is called binding).

Recently, Catalano and Fiore [41] proposed a new primitive called Vector Commitment, which is closely related to zero-knowledge sets [40, 48, 95, 103]. Informally speaking, a vector commitment scheme allows one to commit to an ordered sequence of values $(m_1, \ldots, m_q)$ in such a way that the committer can later open the commitment at specific positions. Furthermore, anyone should not be able to open a commitment to two different values at the same position (this is called position binding). Furthermore, the vector can be required to be hiding. That is, any adversary cannot distinguish whether a commitment was created to a sequence $(m_1, \ldots, m_q)$

or to $(m'_1, \ldots, m'_q)$, even after seeing some openings at some positions. Besides the properties of position binding and hiding, vector commitment needs to be concise, i.e., the size of the commitment string and the opening are both independent of q. In the following, we present a formal definition of vector commitment [41].

Definition 2.1   A vector commitment scheme VC=(VC.KeyGen, VC.Com, VC.Open, VC.Veri, VC.Update, VC.ProofUpdate) consists of the following algorithms:

- VC.KeyGen($1^k, q$): On input the security parameter k and the size $q = poly(k)$ of the committed vector, the key generation algorithm outputs some public parameters PP which also implicitly define the message space $\mathcal{M}$.

- VC.Com$_{PP}(m_1, \cdots, m_q)$: On input a sequence of q messages $(m_1, \cdots, m_q) \in \mathcal{M}^q$, and the public parameters PP, the committing algorithm outputs a commitment string C and an auxiliary information aux.

- VC.Open$_{PP}(m, i, \text{aux})$: This algorithm is run by the committer to produce a proof π_i that m is the i-th committed message.

- VC.Veri$_{PP}(C, m, i, \pi_i)$: The verification algorithm outputs 1 only if π_i is a valid proof that C is a commitment to a sequence $(m_1, \cdots, m_q)$ such that $m = m_i$.

- VC.Update$_{PP}(C, m, i, m')$: This algorithm is run by the original committer who wants to update C by changing the i-th message to m'. It takes as input the old message m at the position i, the new message m', outputs a new commitment C' together with an update information U.

- VC.ProofUpdate$_{PP}(C, U, m', j, \pi_j)$: The algorithm can be run by any user who holds a proof π_j for some message m at the position j w.r.t. C. It allows the user to compute an updated proof π'_j (and the updated commitment C') such that π'_j is valid w.r.t C' which contains m' as the new message at the position i. Basically, the value $U = (m, m', i)$ contains the update information which is needed to compute such values.

2.6   ALGEBRAIC PSEUDORANDOM FUNCTIONS

An algebraic pseudorandom function (PRF) consists of three algorithms $\mathcal{PRF} = \{\text{KeyGen}, F, \text{CFEval}\}$. Given a security parameter 1^n and a parameter $m \in \mathbb{N}$, the algorithm KeyGen determines the domain size of the PRF and outputs a pair $(K, param) \in \mathcal{K}_n$, where $\mathcal{K}_n$ is the key space for security parameter n, K is the secret key of the PRF, and $param$ encodes the public parameters. The algorithm F takes as input a key K, public parameters $param$, an input $x \in \{0, 1\}^m$, and outputs a value $y \in Y$, where Y is some set determined by $param$.

An algebraic pseudorandom function should satisfy the following properties [18]:

- **Algebraic**: $\mathcal{PRF}$ is algebraic if the range Y of $F_K(\cdot)$ for every $n \in \mathbb{N}$ and $(K, param) \in \mathcal{K}_n$ forms an abelian group. Given $param$, the group operation on Y should be efficiently computable.

- **Pseudorandom**: $\mathcal{PRF}$ is pseudorandom if for every PPT adversary A, and every polynomial $m(\cdot)$, there exists a negligible function $neg: \mathbb{N} \to \mathbb{N}$, such that for all $n \in \mathbb{N}$:

$$|\Pr[A^{F_K(\cdot)}(1^n, param) = 1] - \Pr[A^{R(\cdot)}(1^n, param) = 1]| \leq neg(n)$$

where $(K, param) \leftarrow_R \mathsf{KeyGen}(1^n, m(n))$, and $R : \{0,1\}^m \to Y$ is a random function.

- **Closed form efficiency**: Let N be the order of the range sets of F for security parameter n. Let $z = (z_0, \cdots, z_l) \in (\{0,1\}^m)^{l+1}, k \in \mathbb{N}$, and an efficiently computable $h : \mathbb{Z}_N^k \to \mathbb{Z}_N^l$ with $h(x) = \langle h_0(x), \cdots, h_l(x) \rangle$. We say that (h, z) is closed form efficient for $\mathcal{PRF}$ if there exists an algorithm $\mathsf{CFEval}_{h,z}$ such that for every $x \in \mathbb{Z}_N^k$,

$$\mathsf{CFEval}_{h,z}(x, K) = \prod_{i=0}^{l} [F_K(z_i)]^{h_i(x)}$$

and the running time of CFEval is polynomial in n, m, k but sublinear in l. When $z = (0, \cdots, l)$, we will omit it from the subscript, and write $\mathsf{CFEval}_h(x, K)$ instead.

The last condition provides a much more efficient way to compute a "weighted product" of l PRF values. That is, given $(param, h, x, F_K(z))$, one can always compute the value $\prod_{i=1}^{l} [F_K(z_i)]^{h_i(x)}$ in time linear in l (this follows from the algebraic property of the PRF).

In the following, we introduce a concrete construction of small domain algebraic PRFs from strong decisional Diffie-Hellman (SDDH) assumption. Let $\mathcal{G}$ be a computational group scheme. We define $\mathcal{PRF}$ as an algebraic PRF with polynomial sized domains.

- $\mathsf{KeyGen}(1^n, m)$: Generate a group description $(p, g, \mathbb{G}) \leftarrow_R \mathcal{G}(1^n)$, where n is a security parameter. Choose $k_0, k_1 \in_R \mathbb{Z}_p$. Output $param = (m, p, g, \mathbb{G})$, $K = (k_0, k_1)$.

- $F_K(x)$: Interpret x as an integer in $\{0, \cdots, D = 2^m\}$ where D is polynomial in n. Compute and output $g^{k_0 k_1^x}$.

- $\mathsf{CFEval}_h(x, K)$: Define $\mathsf{CFEval}_h(x, K) = g^{\frac{k_0(1 - k_1^{d+1} x^{d+1})}{1 - k_1 x}}$.

We now show an efficient closed form for $\mathcal{PRF}$ for polynomials of the form:

$$p(x) = F_K(0) + F_K(1)x + \cdots + F_K(d)x^d, \text{ where } d \leq D.$$

Let $h : \mathbb{Z}_p \to \mathbb{Z}_p^{d+1}$ be defined as $h(x) \stackrel{\text{def}}{=} (1, x, \cdots, x^d)$. Let $(z_0, \cdots, z_d) = (0, \cdots, d)$. Then we have

$$\mathsf{CFEval}_h(x, K) = \prod_{i=0}^{d} [F_K(z_i)]^{h_i(x)} = \prod_{i=0}^{d} [g^{k_0 k_1^i}]^{x^i} = g^{k_0 \sum_{i=0}^{d} k_1^i x^i} = g^{\frac{k_0(1-k_1^{d+1} x^{d+1})}{1-k_1 x}}.$$

This proves the correctness of $\mathsf{CFEval}_h(x)$.

2.7 BLOOM FILTER

The Bloom filter, proposed by Bloom [24] in 1970, is a space-efficient data structure for approximately representing a large set S subject to insertion operations and membership queries. A Bloom filter (BF) consists of a hash table B containing m single-bit cells which are initially set to 0, together with k random hash functions $h_i : \{0, 1\}^* \to [1, m]$ for $1 \le i \le k$. Note that the hash function is not the traditional one such as SHA-1. In the initial phase, all positions of the array are set to 0. To add an element to the set, feed it to each of the k hash functions and obtain k array positions. Then set the bit value for each position to 1, i.e., $B[h_i(x)].bit = 1$ for $i = 1, 2, \cdots, k$.

In order to test whether an element x in S or not, we must ensure that there is no $i \in \{1, 2 \cdots, k\}$ such that $B[h_i(x)].bit = 0$. That is, if there exists some $i \in \{1, 2 \cdots, k\}$ such that $B[h_i(x)].bit = 0$, then x is definitely not in S. Otherwise, we can deduce that x is a member of S with a probability of false positive.

An instance of Bloom filter is shown in Fig. 2.1. It is easy to see that the element z does not belong to the set S. In the case of element w, though all the corresponding positions are 1, it does not belong to S. It is called as false positive. In [4], the authors analyze the relationship among the size of the Bloom filter m, the number of hash functions k, the number of elements n, and the probability of false positive P_f. Specifically, for given m and n, $P_f = (1 - e^{-kn/m})^k$. Also, when $k = ln2 * (m/n)$, P_f reaches the minimum value $(0.6185)^{m/n}$.

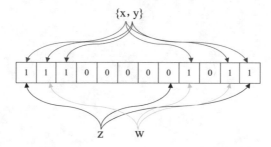

Figure 2.1: A toy Bloom filter construction.

Some variants of Bloom filter consist of the counting Bloom filter (CBF), invertible Bloom filter (IBF) [28, 65]. For example, CBF is a variant of Bloom filter by replacing each *bit* cell of B with a counter cell called *count* (initialized to 0 for each cell). An insertion/deletion of element x amounts to incrementing/decrementing each $B[h_i(x)].count$ by 1 for $i = 1, 2, \cdots, k$. Similarly, testing for the membership of x in S amounts to testing that there is no $i \in \{1, 2 \cdots, k\}$ such that $B[h_i(x)]$.count $= 0$. However, it is still very difficult to find (not just test) the members of a set represented by a CBF.

We believe that these primitives play an important role in designing verifiable database schemes with efficient updates and will present in our future work [54].

CHAPTER 3

Secure Outsourcing of Scientific Computations

In this chapter we focus on secure outsourcing some scientific computations. The theoretical computer science community has devoted considerable attention to the problem of how to securely outsource different kinds of expensive computations. Abadi et al. [2] first proved the impossibility of secure outsourcing an exponential computation while locally doing only polynomial time work. Therefore, it is meaningful only to consider outsourcing expensive polynomial time computations.

Atallah et al. [7] presented a framework for secure outsourcing of scientific computations such as matrix multiplications and quadrature. However, the solution used the disguise technique and thus allowed leakage of private information. Atallah and Li [3] investigated the problem of computing the edit distance between two sequences and presented an efficient protocol to securely outsource sequence comparisons to two servers. Blanton et al. proposed a more efficient scheme for secure outsourcing sequence comparisons [23]. Benjamin and Atallah [8] addressed the problem of secure outsourcing for widely applicable linear algebra computations. However, the proposed protocols required the expensive operations of homomorphic encryptions. Atallah and Frikken [1] further studied this problem and gave improved protocols based on Shamir's secret sharing. Some other works [93, 100] also used Shamir's secret sharing to perform homomorphic computations over the cloud. Trivially, the protocols based on secret sharing require at least two non-colluding servers. Wang et al. [123] presented efficient mechanisms for secure outsourcing of linear programming computations. However, the solution requires matrix-matrix operations (cubic-time computational burden). Recently, Wang et al. [126] proposed a secure outsourcing mechanism for solving large-scale systems of linear equations based on the iterative methods. However, it requires multi-round interactions between the client and the cloud server.

In the following, we introduce the protocols for securely outsourcing matrix multiplication, matrix inversion, and large-scale system of linear equations, respectively.

3.1 MATRIX MULTIPLICATION

In this section, we introduce two classical protocols for outsourcing matrix multiplication [7]. That is, given two $n \times n$ matrices M_1 and M_2, the goal of the client C is to compute the product $M_1 M_2$. Since the inputs should not be revealed to the server S, the main trick in these protocols is how to efficiently disguise the matrices. In some references, the disguising is also-called blinding (a typical example is blind signature [33]). From the viewpoint of cryptography, blinding is actually a kind of one-time encryption, i.e., the blind factor should not be re-used.

Now we consider the problem of matrix multiplication and we only foucs on the dense matrix. A straightforward solution to disguise a matrix is to multiply a random matrix. However, the problem is that the computational complexity for multiplying two random $n \times n$ dense matrices is $O(n^3)$. Note that we assume that the resource-limited client cannot perform $O(n^3)$ operations. Atallah et al. [7] presented the following two ways to efficiently disguise a dense matrix by using the random permutations and (special) sparse matrices. More precisely, the sparse matrices (e.g., P_1 below) in the constructions are not random chosen sparse ones. Actually, they are the product of some elementary matrices! Also, the inverse of these matrices could be computed easily, while the sparse matrices used in [51] are random ones and computing the inverse is a prohibitively expensive task for the client. Besides, another issue is that the client cannot verify the validity of result in both schemes [7]. Thus, the construction should be given in the honest but curious model.

3.1.1 A BASIC SOLUTION

Let $\delta_{x,y}$ be the Kronecker delta function that equals 1 if $x = y$ and 0 if $x \neq y$. The first outsourcing protocol consists of the following steps:

1. C generates three random permutations π_1, π_2, and π_3 of the integers $\{1, 2, \cdots, n\}$, and three sets of non-zero random numbers $\{\alpha_1, \alpha_2, \cdots, \alpha_n\}$, $\{\beta_1, \beta_2, \cdots, \beta_n\}$ and $\{\gamma_1, \gamma_2, \cdots, \gamma_n\}$. Define $P_1(i, j) = \alpha_i \delta_{\pi_1(i),j}$, $P_2(i, j) = \beta_i \delta_{\pi_2(i),j}$, $P_3(i, j) = \gamma_i \delta_{\pi_3(i),j}$. Note that these matrices are readily invertible, e.g., $P_1^{-1}(i, j) = (\alpha_i)^{-1} \delta_{\pi_1^{-1}(i),j}$.

2. C computes the matrices $X = P_1 M_1 P_2^{-1}$ and $Y = P_2 M_2 P_3^{-1}$, where $X(i, j) = (\alpha_i/\beta_j) M_1(\pi_1(i), \pi_2(j))$, and $Y(i, j) = (\beta_i/\gamma_j) M_2(\pi_2(i), \pi_3(j))$.

3. C sends X and Y to S. Then S computes the product

$$Z = XY = (P_1 M_1 P_2^{-1})(P_2 M_2 P_3^{-1}) = P_1 M_1 M_2 P_3^{-1}$$

and sends Z back.

4. C computes the matrix $M_1 M_2 = P_1^{-1} Z P_3$ locally in $O(n^2)$ time.

In order to determine M_1 (or M_2), S must guess two permutations (from $(n!)^2$ possible choices) and $3n$ numbers ($\alpha_i, \beta_i, \gamma_i$). Thus, it is secure enough in many applications when n is sufficiently large (while not in the sense of cryptography).[1] Also, the disguise requires $O(n^2)$ local computation, and the outsourced computations require $O(n^3)$ operations.

Note that this disguise technique is not a perfect disguise since the data in the matrix is not fully blind. The matrix M_1 is transformed into X as $X = P_1 M_1 P_2^{-1}$, where $X(i, j) =$

---

[1]This indicates that the disguise could not achieve the cryptographic security since n is at most polynomial size.

$(\alpha_i / \beta_j) M_1(\pi_1(i), \pi_2(j))$. The non-zero number a in M_1 will be transformed into $\alpha_i a / \beta_j$, and the location is changed according to the two random permutations $(\pi_1(i), \pi_2(j))$. However, the number 0 in M_1 is still 0 even though the location is changed. Hence, this disguise technique cannot protect the number 0 in M_1.

3.1.2   AN ENHANCED SOLUTION

The second outsourcing protocol enhances the security compared with the first one (while the efficiency is reduced). The main trick consists of two steps: The first one is to hide a matrix by the sparse random matrices P_i or their inverse P_i^{-1} just as above. The second one is to hide the resulting matrix by adding a dense random matrix.

1. C computes matrices $X = P_1 M_1 P_2^{-1}$ and $Y = P_2 M_2 P_3^{-1}$ as in the first outsourcing protocol in Section 3.1.1

2. C generates four random numbers $\beta, \gamma, \beta', \gamma'$ such that

$$(\beta + \gamma)(\beta' + \gamma')(\gamma'\beta - \gamma\beta') \neq 0.$$

3. C selects two random $n \times n$ matrices S_1 and S_2 and computes the six matrices

$$X + S_1, \ \beta X - \gamma S_1, \ \beta' X - \gamma' S_1,$$
$$Y + S_2, \ \beta Y - \gamma S_2, \ \beta' Y - \gamma' S_2.$$

   Then C outsources the three matrix multiplications to S

$$W = (X + S_1)(Y + S_2)$$
$$U = (\beta X - \gamma S_1)(\beta Y - \gamma S_2)$$
$$U' = (\beta' X - \gamma' S_1)(\beta' Y - \gamma' S_2)$$

   which are returned.

4. C computes the matrices

$$V = (\beta + \gamma)^{-1}(U + \beta\gamma W)$$
$$V' = (\beta' + \gamma')^{-1}(U' + \beta'\gamma' W)$$

   Observe that $V = \beta XY + \gamma S_1 S_2$ and $V' = \beta' XY + \gamma' S_1 S_2$.

5. C computes $XY = (\gamma'\beta - \gamma\beta')^{-1}(\gamma'V - \gamma V')$.

6. C computes $M_1 M_2 = P_1^{-1} XY P_3$.

3.2 MATRIX INVERSION

In this section, we introduce a secure outsourcing protocol for matrix inversion which uses the secure matrix multiplication protocol above as a subroutine [7]. The aim of this protocol is to compute the inversion matrix M^{-1} of an $n \times n$ matrix M .

1. C selects a random $n \times n$ matrix N. If N is non-invertible, then the following Step 4 below sends us back to Step 1.

2. The client outsources $\hat{M} = MN$ to S using the secure matrix multiplication protocol in Section 3.1. Trivially, the server could know neither M, nor N, nor $\hat{M}$.

3. C generates five matrices P_1, P_2, P_3, P_4, P_5 using the same method as in Section 3.1. That is, $P_1(i, j) = a_i \delta_{\pi_1(i).j}, P_2(i, j) = b_i \delta_{\pi_2(i).j}, P_3(i, j) = c_i \delta_{\pi_3(i).j}, P_4(i, j) = d_i \delta_{\pi_4(i).j}$, and $P_5(i, j) = e_i \delta_{\pi_5(i).j}$, where $\pi_1, \pi_2, \pi_3, \pi_4, \pi_5$ are random permutations, and where the a_i, b_i, c_i, d_i, e_i are random numbers. C computes the matrices

$$Q = P_1 \hat{M} P_2^{-1}; R = P_3 N P_4^{-1}.$$

4. C outsources the computation of Q^{-1} to S. If it succeeds, S returns Q^{-1}. Otherwise, S returns "non-inertible." Then we know that at least one of N or M (possibly both) is non-invertible. C performs the following procedure:

   - C firstly obtains $\hat{N} = N_1 N N_2$ where N_1 and N_2 are matrices already known to be invertible and then outsources $\hat{N}$ to the server for inverting. Note that the computation of $\hat{N}$ should also be outsourced to S by running the subroutine of matrix multiplication twice.

   - If S can invert $\hat{N}$ (note that C really cares not about the value $\hat{N}$ but whether $\hat{N}$ is invertible or not), then N is invertible. Hence, we know that M is not invertible. Otherwise, $\hat{N}$ is not invertible and thus N is not invertible. In this case, return to Step 1.

5. C computes the matrix $T = P_4 P_2^{-1} Q^{-1} P_1 P_5^{-1}$ and outsources S the computation of $Z = RT$ using the secure matrix multiplication protocol in Section 3.1.

6. C computes $M^{-1} = P_3^{-1} Z P_5$ since $Z = P_3 M^{-1} P_5^{-1}$.

The security of the above protocol follows from the facts that the calculations of $\hat{M}$ and Z are done using secure matrix multiplication. Also, the usage of matrices $P_1, \ldots, P_5$ for computing Q, R, T is never repeated (that is, the random blinding factor should be never re-used). Another important fact is that the random permutations and numbers used for secure matrix multiplication subroutine in Steps 2 and 5 must be independently generated from Step 3.

One disadvantage of this protocol is that it must run the subroutine of matrix multiplication four times and matrix inversion (at least) one time. That is, it requires at least five rounds of interaction between C and S. This is really inefficient for real applications. Another disadvantage of this protocol is that C must choose lots of random permutations and numbers (even worse in the case of non-invertible N). Finally, we point out that the protocol is only valid under the assumption of honest-but-curious server. C could not check the validity of results given by S in Steps 2, 4, and 5.

3.3 LARGE-SCALE LINEAR EQUATIONS SYSTEMS

The large-scale system of linear equations $\mathbf{Ax} = \mathbf{b}$ is one of the most basic algebraic problems in the scientific community [20, 68]. There are a lot of real-world computation problems that would result in a large-scale system of linear equations with up to thousands or even millions of unknown variables. For example, a typical double-precision $50,000 \times 50,000$ system matrix resulted from electromagnetic application would easily occupy up to 20 GBytes storage space. Therefore, the storage requirements for such a system coefficient matrix may easily exceed the available memory of the customer's computing device, such as a modern portable laptop. Besides, it is inefficient to perform computations on such a huge system coefficient matrix. Plenty of researchers have devoted a considerable amount of effort on seeking efficient algorithms for the task.

The problem for securely outsourcing large-scale systems of linear equations can be formulated as follows: The client C seeks the solution to a large-scale system of linear equations $\mathbf{Ax} = \mathbf{b}$, where $\mathbf{A} \in \mathbb{R}^{n \times n}$ is a real coefficient matrix with rank n, and $\mathbf{b} \in \mathbb{R}^n$ is a coefficient vector. Due to the lack of computing resources, it could be infeasible for C to carry out such expensive computation as $O(n^\rho)$ for $2 < \rho \leq 3$ locally. Therefore, C will outsource the computation workloads to cloud server S in a pay-per-use manner. Note that we only consider the case that $\mathbf{A}$ is a general nonsingular dense matrix. For the case of (extremely) sparse matrices, there may be other more efficient methods to solve the linear equations.

Atallah et al. [7] presented an outsourcing protocol for a system of linear equations based on the above outsourcing techniques of matrix multiplication and inversion. The main trick is to hide the solutions into a matrix through random permutations and scalings and then use the technique of matrix inversion. We give a brief overview as below.

1. C selects a random $n \times n$ matrix B and a random number $j \in \{1, 2, \cdots, n\}$. Then, C replaces the j-th column of B by $\mathbf{b}$, i.e., $B = [B_1, \cdots, B_{j-1}, \mathbf{b}, B_{j+1}, \cdots, B_n]$.

2. C generates three matrices P_1, P_2, P_3 as in Section 3.1. That is, $P_1(i, j) = a_i \delta_{\pi_1(i), j}$, $P_2(i, j) = b_i \delta_{\pi_2(i), j}$, $P_3(i, j) = c_i \delta_{\pi_3(i), j}$, where π_1, π_2, π_3 are random permutations, and where the a_i, b_i, c_i are random numbers.

3. C computes the matrices

$$\hat{A} = P_1 A P_2^{-1}; \ \hat{B} = P_1 B P_3^{-1}.$$

4. C outsources $\hat{A}, \hat{B}$ to S in order to get the solution of the linear system $\hat{A}\hat{X} = \hat{B}$. If the server returns that $\hat{A}$ is singular, then C also returns that A is singular. Otherwise S returns

$$\hat{X} = \hat{A}^{-1}\hat{B}.$$

5. C compute $X = P_2^{-1}\hat{X}P_3$ which equals $A^{-1}B$.

6. The answer x is the j-th column of X, i.e., $x = X_j$.

The security of this process follows from the fact that $\mathbf{b}$ is hidden through the expansion to a matrix B, and then A and B are hidden through random scalings and permutations. Also, it uses the interactive matrix inversion in Section 3.2 as a building block, and thus the scheme is also interactive and complicated.

3.3.1 NEW SECURE OUTSOURCING PROTOCOL

In the following, we introduce a new protocol **LE** [51] for securely outsourcing large-scale systems of linear equations in the fully malicious model. That is, the computation is delegated to only one server who may be lazy, curious, and dishonest. The main trick is to use two random *sparse* matrices to hide **A**. More precisely, C chooses two random sparse matrices $\mathbf{M}, \mathbf{N} \in \mathbb{R}^{n \times n}$ and computes $\mathbf{T} = \mathbf{MAN}$. The reason to use sparse matrices is that the computational complexity for two dense matrices' multiplication is $O(n^3)$. Now we analyze the case that a sparse matrix $\mathbf{M}$ multiplies a dense one $\mathbf{A}$. Without loss of generality, we assume that there are at most λ ($\lambda << n$) non-zero elements for each row of $\mathbf{M}$. Obviously, it takes at most λn^2 multiplications to calculate $\mathbf{MA}$ and the computational complexity is $O(n^2)$ since the constant $\lambda << n$. Thus, C can efficiently compute $\mathbf{T} = \mathbf{MAN}$ with the complexity of $O(n^2)$.

The input of **LE** is a coefficient vector $\mathbf{b} \in \mathbb{R}^n$ and a coefficient matrix $\mathbf{A} \in \mathbb{R}^{n \times n}$. The output of **LE** is a coefficient vector $\mathbf{x} \in \mathbb{R}^n$ such that $\mathbf{Ax} = \mathbf{b}$. The proposed protocol **LE** is given as follows:

1. **KeyGen**$(\mathsf{F}, \lambda) \to (PK, SK)$: Given the security parameter λ and the target function F : $\mathbf{Ax} = \mathbf{b}$, C picks a random blinding coefficient vector $\mathbf{r} \in \mathbb{R}^n$ and two random blinding sparse matrices $\mathbf{M}, \mathbf{N} \in \mathbb{R}^{n \times n}$. Note that $(\mathbf{M}, \mathbf{N}, \mathbf{r})$ are one-time blinding factors that must be generated each time for different linear equations. Then, we have $PK = n$ and $SK = (\mathbf{M}, \mathbf{N}, \mathbf{r})$.

2. **ProbGen**$_{SK}(x) \to (\sigma_x, \tau_x)$: Given the input $x = (\mathbf{A}, \mathbf{b})$, C firstly computes $\mathbf{c} = \mathbf{Ar} + \mathbf{b}$. Trivially, the original linear equations can be rewritten as $\mathbf{A}(\mathbf{x} + \mathbf{r}) = \mathbf{c}$. Then, C computes $\mathbf{T} = \mathbf{MAN}$ and $\mathbf{d} = \mathbf{Mc}$. Without loss of generality, we denote $\mathbf{y} = \mathbf{N}^{-1}(\mathbf{x} + \mathbf{r})$, where

N^{-1} is the inverse of matrix N. We emphasize that *no* party needs to compute N^{-1} in this algorithm. It appears here only for representing the form of y. Note that

$$Ty = MAN \cdot N^{-1}(x + r) = MA(x + r) = Mc = d.$$

Therefore, $\sigma_x = (T, d)$, and $\tau_x = (M, N, r)$.

3. **Compute**$_{PK}(\sigma_x) \to \sigma_y$: C sends σ_x to S, and S responds with the solution $\sigma_y = y$ such that $Ty = d$.

4. **Verify**$_{SK}(\tau_x, \sigma_y) \to y \cup \perp$: C verifies whether the equations $Ty = d$ hold. If not, C outputs $\perp$ and claims the misbehavior of S. Otherwise, C computes $x = Ny - r$ as the result of function $y = F(x)$. The computational complexity for the verification is still $O(n^2)$. This is due to the fact that it requires at most n^2 multiplications to compute Ty for any (even totally dense) matrix T and any coefficient vector y. Furthermore, C can detect the misbehavior of S with the probability 1.

The protocol **LE** only requires one round of communication between C and S. This is different from Wang et al.'s protocol [126] that requires multi-round communication between C and S. More precisely, it may require dozens (or even hundreds) of iterations for a different matrix A by using the iteration methods. As a result, it also requires dozens (or even hundreds) of rounds of communications between C and S. Therefore, the scheme could be impractical for real-world applications.

Some further (implicit) observations on **LE** are listed as below:

1. Note that the sparse matrices M and N must be invertible (also-called nonsingular). By Lévy-Desplanques Theorem (see theorem 6.1.10 of [83]), we know that a strictly diagonally dominant matrix $A \in \mathbb{R}^{n \times n}$ is definitely nonsingular. Therefore, in the real applications, we could choose sparse and row diagonally dominant matrix A such that $\sum_{j \neq i} |a_{ij}| < |a_{ii}|$ for all $1 \leq i \leq n$. On the other hand, neither C nor S needs to compute N^{-1}. Otherwise, the protocol **LE** is totally impractical. The reason is twofold: Firstly, though N is a sparse matrix, the inverse matrix N^{-1} may be extremely dense. As a result, the computation and storage cost for N^{-1} will be very expensive. Secondly, the computation complexity of N^{-1} is $O(n^3)$ if we use the naive Gaussian elimination or Gauss-Jordan elimination method.[2] This contradicts the assumption that C cannot carry out such expensive computation as $O(n^\rho)$ for $2 < \rho \leq 3$.

2. Given T and d, S can solve the systems of linear equations $Ty = d$ in any desired methods such as elimination methods, decomposition (factorization) methods, iterative methods,

---

[2]The complexity of the Strassen algorithm is still $O(n^{2.807})$. Coppersmith and Winograd presented the state-of-the-art record which stands at $O(n^{2.376})$. However, the programming of the two algorithms is so awkward and thus neither of them is suitable for practical applications.

etc. However, as pointed out in [20], for the systems comprising hundreds of millions or even billions of equations in as many unknowns, iterative methods may be the only option available (unless the iteration does not converge). Furthermore, we argue that it does not require the interactive protocol between C and S in our proposed solution. As a result, S can efficiently compute $\mathbf{y}$ using the iterative methods.

3.3.2   SECURITY ANALYSIS

In the following, we prove that the algorithms (C, S) in **LE** can achieve the three security properties defined in Section 1.3.

Theorem 3.1   *In the fully malicious model, the algorithms (C, S) in **LE** achieve the privacy for A, b, and x.*

Proof.   We first prove the privacy for input $\mathbf{b}$ and output $\mathbf{x}$ of **LE**. Note that the adversary $\mathcal{A}$ can only know $\mathbf{T}$ and $\mathbf{d}$ throughout the whole algorithm **LE**. Besides, we have $\mathbf{b} = \mathbf{M}^{-1}\mathbf{d} - \mathbf{Ar}$, and $\mathbf{x} = \mathbf{Ny} - \mathbf{r}$. Since $\mathbf{r}$ is a random blinding coefficient vector in $\mathbb{R}^n$, both $\mathbf{b}$ and $\mathbf{x}$ are blinded by $\mathbf{r}$ in the sense of computational indistinguishability.

We then prove the privacy for input $\mathbf{A}$ of **LE**. Let $\mathbf{M} = (m_{ij}), \mathbf{N} = (n_{ij}), \mathbf{M}' = (m'_{ij})$, and $\mathbf{N}' = (n'_{ij})$ be four random nonsingular sparse matrices generated by C. Given two nonsingular dense matrices $\mathbf{A} = (a_{ij})$ and $\mathbf{A}' = (a'_{ij})$ which are chosen by the adversary $\mathcal{A}$, C computes $\mathbf{T} = \mathbf{MAN} = (t_{ij})$ and $\mathbf{T}' = \mathbf{M}'\mathbf{A}'\mathbf{N}' = (t'_{ij})$, where

$$t_{ij} = \sum_{l=1}^{n}\sum_{k=1}^{n} m_{ik} \cdot a_{kl} \cdot n_{lj}$$

and

$$t'_{ij} = \sum_{l=1}^{n}\sum_{k=1}^{n} m'_{ik} \cdot a'_{kl} \cdot n'_{lj}.$$

Note that the numerical value and position of all non-zero elements of four matrices $\mathbf{M}, \mathbf{N}, \mathbf{M}'$, and $\mathbf{N}'$ are randomly chosen by C, thus the two values t_{ij} and t'_{ij} are computationally indistinguishable. Thus, the advantage of $\mathcal{A}$ to distinguish between $\mathbf{T}$ and $\mathbf{T}'$ is negligible.   □

Remark 1. Note that we currently cannot prove the privacy for any input $\mathbf{A}$ of **LE** (this is not essential in **LE** since we only focus on the case that $\mathbf{A}$ is a nonsingular dense matrix). For example, if the adversary $\mathcal{A}$ chooses a nonsingular matrix $\mathbf{A}$ and a singular one $\mathbf{A}'$, then he can distinguish between $\mathbf{T} = \mathbf{MAN}$ and $\mathbf{T}' = \mathbf{M}'\mathbf{A}'\mathbf{N}'$ with an overwhelming probability since $\mathbf{T}'$ is always singular.

Even in some special case that both $\mathbf{A}$ and $\mathbf{A}'$ are nonsingular, e.g., let $\mathbf{A}$ be a nonsingular dense matrix and $\mathbf{A}'$ be the identity matrix that is extremely sparse, it seems to be difficult to efficiently distinguish between $\mathbf{T}$ and $\mathbf{T}'$ with a non-negligible probability.[3] Actually, there is a paradox between the privacy and efficiency of the outsourcing scheme for any input $\mathbf{A}$. More precisely, in order to achieve privacy for any input $\mathbf{A}$, the blinding matrix $\mathbf{M}$ (and $\mathbf{N}$) for masking $\mathbf{A}$ should also be a random one (and thus may be a dense one). However, it requires $O(n^3)$ computational overhead to compute $\mathbf{T}$ (or $\mathbf{T}'$) in this case. This makes the outsourcing totally meaningless. We left it as an open problem.

Theorem 3.2 *In the fully malicious model, the algorithms (C, S) in **LE** are an $O(\frac{1}{n})$-efficient implementation of **LE**.*

Proof. In the proposed algorithm **LE**, C needs to perform four matrix-vector multiplication (we omit the vector-addition operations), which takes $O(n^2)$ computations. Besides, C also needs to compute $\mathbf{T} = \mathbf{MAN}$, which also takes $O(n^2)$ computations. On the other hand, it takes $O(n^3)$ computations in order to solve the linear equations directly. Therefore, the algorithms (C, S) are an $O(\frac{1}{n})$-efficient implementation of **LE**. □

Theorem 3.3 *In the fully malicious model, the algorithms (C, S) in **LE** are a 1-checkable implementation of **LE**.*

Proof. Given a solution $\mathbf{y}$, C can verify whether the equations $\mathbf{Ty} = \mathbf{d}$ hold efficiently because the computational complexity for $\mathbf{Ty}$ is $O(n^2)$. Therefore, if S misbehaves during any execution of **LE**, it will be detected by C with probability $\beta = 1$. □

---

[3]Note that the product of extremely sparse matrices can be complete dense [132], thus C could choose suitable $\mathbf{M}'$ and $\mathbf{N}'$ to ensure that $\mathbf{T}' = \mathbf{M}'\mathbf{N}'$ is a dense matrix. Obviously, it is impossible to distinguish $\mathbf{T}$ and $\mathbf{T}'$ only based on the sparsity of a matrix.

CHAPTER 4

Secure Outsourcing of Cryptographic Operations

In this chapter, we consider the problem of secure outsourcing expensive cryptographic operations in public key cryptography (PKC).

The idea of PKC was introduced by Diffie and Hellman [63] 40 years ago (just the same as my age) and it is really a milestone in the history of cryptology. Plenty of PKC schemes were broken soon after their birth (even some inventors may claim that their constructions could not be broken forever!). Nowadays, only two kinds of number-theoretic-based cryptographic systems are believed to be secure and efficient, i.e., the integer-factorization-based system and discrete-logarithm-based system. Some well-known concrete constructions include the RSA system, El-Gamal system, ECC system, etc.

The first decade belongs to the RSA system, one of the most commonly used PKC systems in the world. Many cryptographers presented much security analysis on the RSA (see Boneh's survey [21]), however, no efficient attacks are successful if we choose the parameters of RSA carefully. The second decade belongs to the elliptic curve cryptography (ECC) system, which was invented by Koblitz and Miller in 1985. Compared to the RSA system, one significant advantage of the ECC system is to offer the same level of security with much shorter parameters. For example, a 160-bit ECC key offers more or less the same level of security as a 1,024-bit RSA key [94]. Note that the main operation in both RSA and ECC systems is the exponentiation modulo a very large integer. As Goldwasser and Micali pointed out, "even schemes like RSA are considered too slow for many practical applications. In particular, these signature schemes require performing modular exponentiation with a large modulus..." [66]. That is, the practicality of PKC schemes is closely related to the efficiency of modular exponentiation.

The next decade is the time of bilinear pairings, which initiated some completely new fields in cryptography. Due to this new powerful tool, it became possible to realize many cryptographic primitives that were previously unknown or impractical, such as one-round tripartite key agreement protocol, ID-based encryption schemes, and short signature schemes. However, the computations of modular exponentiation and bilinear pairings are considered to be prohibitively expensive operations in embedded devices, such as RFID tag, and smart cards. Thus, the problem of securely outsourcing such expensive computations has been well studied in the cryptography community.

In 1992, Chaum and Pedersen [34] introduced the notion of "wallets with observers," a piece of secure hardware installed on the client's computer to perform some expensive computations—a prototype of outsourcing computation. In 2005, Hohenberger and Lysyanskaya [82] proposed the first outsource-secure algorithm for modular exponentiations based on the two previous approaches of precomputation [31, 115] and server-aided computation [71, 97]. In their algorithm, the client needs to do some logic split on the parameters before sending them to the two untrusted servers. Depending on the results that are returned by the two servers, the client can verify the correctness of the result with probability $\frac{1}{2}$. Chevallier-Mames et al. [37] presented the first algorithm for secure delegation of elliptic-curve pairings based on an untrusted server model. Besides, the client could detect any failures with probability 1 if the server misbehaves. However, an obvious disadvantage of the algorithm is that the client should carry out some other expensive operations such as point multiplications (or called scalar multiplications) and exponentiations. Therefore, the algorithm is not practical for real-world applications in this sense.

4.1   SECURITY DEFINITIONS

Informally, we say that C securely outsources some computations to S, and (C, S) is an *outsource-secure* implementation of a cryptographic algorithm Alg if (1) C and S implement Alg, i.e., Alg $= C^S$ and (2) suppose that C is given oracle access to an adversary S' (instead of S) that records all of its computation over time and tries to act maliciously, S' cannot learn anything interesting about the input and output of $C^{S'}$.

In the following, we introduce the formal definitions for secure outsourcing of a cryptographic algorithm [82].

Definition 4.1   (Algorithm with outsource-I/O) An algorithm Alg obeys the outsource input/output specification if it takes five inputs, and produces three outputs. The first three inputs are generated by an honest party, and are classified by how much the adversary $A = (E, S')$ knows about them, where E is the adversarial environment that submits adversarially chosen inputs to Alg, and S' is the adversarial software operating in place of oracle S. The first input is called the honest, secret input, which is unknown to both E and S'; the second is called the honest, protected input, which may be known by E, but is protected from S'; and the third is called the honest, unprotected input, which may be known by both E and S. In addition, there are two adversarially chosen inputs generated by the environment E: the adversarial, protected input, which is known to E, but protected from S'; and the adversarial, unprotected input, which may be known by E and S. Similarly, the first output is called secret, which is unknown to both E and S'; the second is protected, which may be known to E, but not S'; and the third is unprotected, which may be known by both parties of A.

The following definition of outsource-security ensures that the malicious environment E cannot gain any knowledge of the secret inputs and outputs of C^S, even if C uses the malicious software S' written by E.

Definition 4.2   (**Outsource-security**) Let Alg be an algorithm with outsource I/O. A pair of algorithms (C, S) is said to be an outsource-secure implementation of Alg if:

1. Correctness: C^S is a correct implementation of Alg.

2. Security: For all probabilistic polynomial-time adversaries $A = (E, S')$, there exist probabilistic expected polynomial-time simulators (S_1, S_2) such that the following pairs of random variables are computationally indistinguishable.

   - Pair One. $EVIEW_{real} \sim EVIEW_{ideal}$:

     - The view that the adversarial environment E obtains by participating in the following *real* process:

$$EVIEW^i_{real} = \{(istate^i, x^i_{hs}, x^i_{hp}, x^i_{hu}) \leftarrow I(1^k, istate^{i-1});$$
$$(estate^i, j^i, x^i_{ap}, x^i_{au}, stop^i) \leftarrow E(1^k, EVIEW^{i-1}_{real}, x^i_{hp}, x^i_{hu});$$
$$(tstate^i, ustate^i, y^i_s, y^i_p, y^i_u) \leftarrow T^{U'(ustate^{i-1})}(tstate^{i-1}, x^{j^i}_{hs}, x^{j^i}_{hp}, x^{j^i}_{hu}, x^i_{ap}, x^i_{au}) :$$
$$(estate^i, y^i_p, y^i_u)\}$$

$EVIEW_{real} = EVIEW^i_{real}$ if $stop^i = TRUE$.

The real process proceeds in rounds. In round i, the honest (secret, protected, and unprotected) inputs $(x^i_{hs}, x^i_{hp}, x^i_{hu})$ are picked using an honest, stateful process I to which the environment E does not have access. Then E, based on its view from the last round, chooses (0) the value of its $estate_i$ variable as a way of remembering what it did next time it is invoked; (1) which previously generated honest inputs $(x^i_{hs}, x^i_{hp}, x^i_{hu})$ to give to $C^{S'}$ (note that E can specify the index j^i of these inputs, but not their values); (2) the adversarial, protected input x^i_{ap}; (3) the adversarial, unprotected input x^i_{au}; (4) the Boolean variable $stop^i$ that determines whether round i is the last round in this process. Next, the algorithm $C^{S'}$ is run on the inputs $(tstate^{i-1}, x^{j^i}_{hs}, x^{j^i}_{hp}, x^{j^i}_{hu}, x^i_{ap}, x^i_{au})$, where $tstate^{i-1}$ is C's previously saved state, and produces a new state $tstate^i$ for C, as well as the secret y^i_s, protected y^i_p and unprotected y^i_u outputs. The oracle S' is given its previously saved state, $ustate^{i-1}$, as input, and the current state of S' is saved in the variable $ustate^i$. The view of the real process in round i consists of $estate^i$, and the values y^i_p and y^i_u. The overall view of E in the real process is just its view in the last round (i.e., i for which $stop^i = TRUE$.).

     - The *ideal* process:

$$EVIEW^i_{ideal} = \{(istate^i, x^i_{hs}, x^i_{hp}, x^i_{hu}) \leftarrow I(1^k, istate^{i-1});$$
$$(estate^i, j^i, x^i_{ap}, x^i_{au}, stop^i) \leftarrow E(1^k, EVIEW^{i-1}_{ideal}, x^i_{hp}, x^i_{hu});$$
$$(astate^i, y^i_s, y^i_p, y^i_u) \leftarrow \mathsf{Alg}(astate^{i-1}, x^{j^i}_{hs}, x^{j^i}_{hp}, x^{j^i}_{hu}, x^i_{ap}, x^i_{au});$$
$$(sstate^i, ustate^i, Y^i_p, Y^i_u, rep^i) \leftarrow \mathsf{S}_1^{U'(ustate^{i-1})}(sstate^{i-1}, \cdots, x^{j^i}_{hp}, x^{j^i}_{hu}, x^i_{ap}, x^i_{au}, y^i_p, y^i_u);$$
$$(z^i_p, z^i_u) = rep^i(Y^i_p, Y^i_u) + (1 - rep^i)(y^i_p, y^i_u):$$
$$(estate^i, z^i_p, z^i_u)\}$$

$EVIEW_{ideal.} = EVIEW^i_{ideal}$ if $stop^i = TRUE$.

The ideal process also proceeds in rounds. In the ideal process, we have a stateful simulator S_1 who, shielded from the secret input x^i_{hs}, but given the non-secret outputs that Alg produces when running all the inputs for round i, decides to either output the values (y^i_p, y^i_u) generated by Alg, or replace them with some other values (Y^i_p, Y^i_u). Note that this is captured by having the indicator variable rep^i be a bit that determines whether y^i_p will be replaced with Y^i_p. In doing so, it is allowed to query oracle S'; moreover, S' saves its state as in the real experiment.

- Pair Two. $UVIEW_{real} \sim UVIEW_{ideal}$:

  - The view that the untrusted software S' obtains by participating in the *real* process described in Pair One. $UVIEW_{real} = ustate^i$ if $stop^i = TRUE$.

  - The *ideal* process:

$$UVIEW^i_{ideal} = \{(istate^i, x^i_{hs}, x^i_{hp}, x^i_{hu}) \leftarrow I(1^k, istate^{i-1});$$
$$(estate^i, j^i, x^i_{ap}, x^i_{au}, stop^i) \leftarrow E(1^k, estate^{i-1}, x^i_{hp}, x^i_{hu}, y^{i-1}_p, y^{i-1}_u);$$
$$(astate^i, y^i_s, y^i_p, y^i_u) \leftarrow \mathsf{Alg}(astate^{i-1}, x^{j^i}_{hs}, x^{j^i}_{hp}, x^{j^i}_{hu}, x^i_{ap}, x^i_{au});$$
$$(sstate^i, ustate^i) \leftarrow \mathsf{S}_2^{U'(ustate^{i-1})}(sstate^{i-1}, x^{j^i}_{hu}, x^i_{au}):$$
$$(ustate^i)\}$$

$UVIEW_{ideal} = UVIEW^i_{ideal}$ if $stop^i = TRUE$.

In the ideal process, we have a stateful simulator S_2 who, equipped with only the unprotected inputs (x^i_{hu}, x^i_{au}), queries S'. As before, S' may maintain state.

Definition 4.3 (α-**efficient, secure outsourcing**) A pair of algorithms (C, S) is said to be an α-efficient implementation of Alg if (1) C^S is a correct implementation of Alg and (2) $\forall$ inputs x, the running time of C is no more than an α-multiplicative factor of the running time of Alg.

Definition 4.4 (β-**checkable, secure outsourcing**) A pair of algorithms (C, S) is said to be a β-checkable implementation of Alg if (1) C^S is a correct implementation of Alg and (2) $\forall$ inputs

x, if S' deviates from its advertised functionality during the execution of $C^{S'}(x)$, C will detect the error with probability no less than β.

Definition 4.5   ((α, β)-**outsource-security**) A pair of algorithms (C, S) is said to be an (α, β)-outsource-secure implementation of Alg if it is both α-efficient and β-checkable.

It is worth noting that, depending on the β parameter, a secure outsourcing algorithm may not provide 100 percent checkability (e.g., [49, 82]). In practice, it is very likely that a client will run the outsourcing algorithm many times with the same server. If a server cheats frequently, there is a high chance that it will be caught in some instances of the algorithm. Then the client may seriously punish the server when a cheating is detected. As a result, the server will not find the incentive to cheat in practice. Nevertheless, it is clear that a larger β is always better. However, there is a tradeoff between the efficiency (α) and checkability (β). For instance, a trivial way to improve the value of β is to add a lot of dummy computations to check whether the server is honest or not. This will significantly reduce the efficiency because the server needs to perform a lot of additional computations.

4.2   TWO UNTRUSTED PROGRAM MODEL

Hohenberger and Lysyanskaya [82] first presented the so-called *two untrusted program model* for outsourcing exponentiations modulo a prime. In this model, the adversarial environment E writes the code for two (potentially different) programs $S' = (S'_1, S'_2)$. E then gives this software to C, advertising a functionality that S'_1 and S'_2 may or may not accurately compute, and C installs this software in a manner such that all subsequent communication between any two of E, S'_1, and S'_2 must pass through C. The new adversary attacking C is $\mathcal{A} = (E, S'_1, S'_2)$. Moreover, we assume that at most one of the programs S'_1 and S'_2 deviates from its advertised functionality on a non-negligible fraction of the inputs, while we cannot know which one, and security means that there is a simulator $\mathcal{S}$ for both. This is named the one-malicious version of two untrusted program model (i.e., "one-malicious model" for simplicity) as shown in Fig. 4.1.

The computation model using multiple, possibly dishonest, but physically separated parties has been well studied in the literature [14, 25, 26]. Actually, in real-world applications, it is equivalent to buying two copies of the advertised software from two different vendors and achieving the security as long as one of them is honest.

4.3   SECURE OUTSOURCING OF SINGLE MODULAR EXPONENTIATION

Modular exponentiation is the most basic operation in discrete-logarithm-based cryptographic protocols. However, it has been considered much more expensive for the resource-limited devices such as RFID tags or smart cards. Therefore, it is important to present an efficient method to securely outsource such operations to (untrusted) powerful servers.

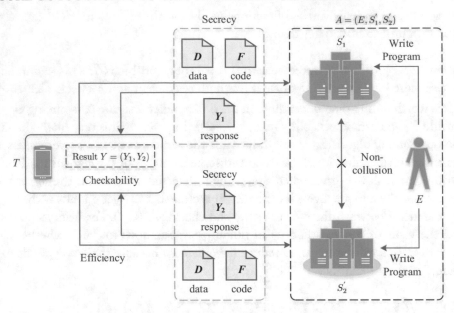

Figure 4.1: One-malicious version of two untrusted program model.

Now we formulate the problem of outsourcing of a single modular exponentiation: the aim of client C is to compute a single modular exponentiation $u^a \mod p$ (for an arbitrary base u and an arbitrary power a), where p is a large prime. Due to limited computational resources, C outsources the operation to two potentially malicious while much more computationally powerful servers S_1 and S_2. An essential requirement is that the adversary A cannot know any useful information about the inputs and outputs of outsourcing algorithm, i.e., (u, a, u^a).

Hohenberger and Lysyanskaya [82] proposed the first outsource-secure modular exponentiation algorithm based on the two previous approaches of precomputation [31, 66, 106, 115] and server-aided computation [12, 71, 97, 128]. The main trick is to use some random blinding factors to logically split the inputs into two random-looking pieces for two untrusted servers. Besides, in the pre-processing phase, C is allowed to invest some one-time expensive computations for a subroutine called *Rand* in order to speed up off-line computation. For each invocation of *Rand*, the inputs are a large prime p, a fixed base $g \in \mathbb{Z}_p^*$, and a random value b, and the outputs are a random, independent pair of the form $(b, g^b \mod p)$.[4] There are two approaches to implement this functionality. One is for a trusted server to compute a table of random, independent pairs in advance and then load it into the memory of C. The other is to apply the well-known preprocessing techniques (e.g., EBPV generator [106]).

---

[4]Though the computation of *Rand* is also to perform a modular exponentiation, it always uses the fixed base g. This is the reason why we cannot just use the subroutine *Rand* to accomplish the outsourcing task. Furthermore, we emphasize that C can never control the output of *Rand* in both approaches, especially the value of b.

Recently, Chen et al. [49] proposed the second secure outsourcing algorithm **Exp** for exponentiation modulo a prime in the one-malicious model. The algorithm is superior to [82] in both efficiency and checkability due to a new splitting and testing trick. The main idea is somewhat similar to the famous "prisoner's dilemma" in game theory. We illustrate it in more detail below.

Suppose that two suspects A and B are arrested and imprisoned while the prosecutors lack sufficient evidence to convict them. Then the prosecutors separate them and each prisoner is in solitary confinement with no means of communicating with the other (i.e., there is either no subliminal channels). Simultaneously, the prosecutors offer them a bargain as follows:

- If A and B both admitted their guilt, each of them serves 10 years in prison.

- If A admitted their guilt while B kept silent, A will be set free and B will serve 30 years in prison (and vice versa).

- If A and B both kept silent, both of them will be serve 1 year in prison.

Trivially, the third case can maximize the common interests of the two suspects. This means that both of them should be dishonest and output the false facts (i.e., neither of them admitted their guilt). However, the experimental results show that the two suspects will betray each other in an overwhelming probability (this means that they output the true facts). This indicates that the probability for two parties to output the same false facts is negligible if they do not collude with each other. In the one-malicious model, the two cloud servers are assumed not to collude with each other. Given the same computation task, the probability for them to output the same invalid results is negligible. Thus, they output either the same valid results or the different invalid results. This fact motivates us to have an idea that we could use some partial computation result to act as a test query in the one-malicious model. Actually, this is the reason why the algorithm [49] could improve Hohenberger and Lysyanskaya's algorithm in both efficiency and checkability.

4.3.1 THE PROPOSED ALGORITHM

Let p, q be two large primes and $q | p - 1$. The input of **Exp** is $a \in \mathbb{Z}_q^*$, and $u \in \mathbb{Z}_p^*$ such that $u^q = 1 \mod p$ (for an arbitrary base u and an arbitrary power a). The output of **Exp** is $u^a \mod p$. Note that a may be secret or (honest/adversarial) protected and u may be (honest/adversarial) protected. Both a and u are computationally blinded to S_1 and S_2. Similar to [82], $S_i(x, y) \to y^x$ also denotes that S_i takes as inputs (x, y) and outputs $y^x \mod p$, where $i = 1, 2$. The proposed algorithm **Exp** is given as follows:

1. To implement this functionality using S_1 and S_2, C firstly runs *Rand* twice to create two blinding pairs (α, g^α) and (β, g^β). We denote $v = g^\alpha \mod p$ and $\mu = g^\beta \mod p$.

2. The main trick is a more efficient solution to logically split u and a into random looking pieces that can be computed by S_1 and S_2. The first logical divisions are

$$u^a = (vw)^a = g^{a\alpha} w^a = g^\beta g^\gamma w^a \mod p,$$

where $w = u/v \mod p$ and $\gamma = a\alpha - \beta \mod q$.

The second logical divisions are

$$u^a = g^\beta g^\gamma w^a = g^\beta g^\gamma w^{k+l} = g^\beta g^\gamma w^k w^l \mod p,$$

where $l = a - k \mod q$.

3. Next, C runs *Rand* to obtain three pairs (t_1, g^{t_1}), (t_2, g^{t_2}), and (t_3, g^{t_3}).

4. C queries S_1 in random order as

   $S_1(t_2/t_1, g^{t_1}) \to g^{t_2}$;

   $S_1(\gamma/t_3, g^{t_3}) \to g^\gamma$;

   $S_1(l, w) \to w^l$.

   Similarly, C queries S_2 in random order as

   $S_2(t_2/t_1, g^{t_1}) \to g^{t_2}$;

   $S_2(\gamma/t_3, g^{t_3}) \to g^\gamma$;

   $S_2(k, w) \to w^k$.

5. Finally, C checks that both S_1 and S_2 produce the correct outputs, i.e., $g^{t_2} = S_1(t_2/t_1, g^{t_1}) = S_2(t_2/t_1, g^{t_1})$ and $S_1(\gamma/t_3, g^{t_3}) = S_2(\gamma/t_3, g^{t_3})$. If not, C outputs "error"; otherwise, C can compute $u^a = \mu g^\gamma w^k w^l$.

Remark 2. In the one-malicious model, the equation $S_1(\gamma/t_3, g^{t_3}) = S_2(\gamma/t_3, g^{t_3})$ implies both S_1 and S_2 produce the correct g^γ. Therefore, the partial computation result g^γ also plays the role of a test query. This is slightly different from the technique in [82] while it indeed improves the efficiency and checkability of the computations.

4.3.2   SECURITY ANALYSIS

Theorem 4.6   *In the one-malicious model, the algorithms $(C, (S_1, S_2))$ are an outsource-secure implementation of **Exp**, where the input (a, u) may be honest, secret; or honest, protected; or adversarial, protected.*

Proof. The proof is similar to [82]. The correctness is trivial and we only focus on security. Let $\mathcal{A} = (E, S_1', S_2')$ be a PPT adversary that interacts with a PPT algorithm C in the one-malicious model.

Firstly, we prove Pair One $EVIEW_{real} \sim EVIEW_{ideal}$:

If the input (a, u) is anything other than honest, secret, then the simulator S_1 behaves the same way as in the real execution. If (a, u) is an honest, secret input, then the simulator S_1 behaves as follows: on receiving the input on round i, S_1 ignores it and instead makes three random queries of the form (α_j, β_j) to both S_1' and S_2'. S_1 randomly tests two outputs (i.e., $\beta_j^{\alpha_j}$) from each program. If an error is detected, S_1 saves all states and outputs $Y_p^i=$"error," $Y_u^i=\varnothing$, $rep^i=1$ (i.e., the output for ideal process is $(estate^i,$ "error," $\varnothing)$). If no error is detected, S_1 checks the remaining two outputs. If all checks pass, S_1 outputs $Y_p^i=\varnothing$, $Y_u^i=\varnothing$, $rep^i=0$ (i.e., the output for ideal process is $(estate^i, y_p^i, y_u^i)$); otherwise, S_1 selects a random element r and outputs $Y_p^i=r$, $Y_u^i=\varnothing$, $rep^i=1$ (i.e., the output for ideal process is $(estate^i, r, \varnothing)$). In either case, S_1 saves the appropriate states. The input distributions to (S_1', S_2') in the real and ideal experiments are computationally indistinguishable. In the ideal experiment, the inputs are chosen uniformly at random. In the real experiment, each part of all three queries that C makes to any one program is independently re-randomized and thus computationally indistinguishable from random. If (S_1', S_2') are honest in round i, then $EVIEW_{real}^i \sim EVIEW_{ideal}^i$ (this is because $C^{(S_1', S_2')}$ perfectly executes **Exp** in the real experiment and S_1 simulates with the same outputs in the ideal experiment, i.e., $rep^i=0$). If one of (S_1', S_2') is dishonest in the round i, then it will be detected by both C and S_1 with probability $\frac{2}{3}$, resulting in an output of "error"; otherwise, the output of **Exp** is corrupted (with probability $\frac{1}{3}$). In the real experiment, the three outputs generated by (S_1', S_2') are multiplied together along with a random value. In the ideal experiment, S_1 also simulates with a random value r. Thus, $EVIEW_{real}^i \sim EVIEW_{ideal}^i$ even when one of (S_1', S_2') is dishonest. By the hybrid argument, we conclude that $EVIEW_{real} \sim EVIEW_{ideal}$.

Secondly, we prove Pair Two $UVIEW_{real} \sim UVIEW_{ideal}$:

The simulator S_2 always behaves as follows: on receiving the input on round i, S_2 ignores it and instead makes three random queries of the form (α_j, β_j) to both S_1' and S_2'. Then S_2 saves its states and the states of (S_1', S_2'). E can easily distinguish between these real and ideal experiments (note that the output in the ideal experiment is never corrupted). However, E cannot communicate this information to (S_1', S_2'). This is because in the round i of the real experiment, C always re-randomizes its inputs to (S_1', S_2'). In the ideal experiment, S_2 always generates random, independent queries for (S_1', S_2'). Thus, for each round i we have $UVIEW_{real}^i \sim UVIEW_{ideal}^i$. By the hybrid argument, we conclude that $UVIEW_{real} \sim UVIEW_{ideal}$. $\qquad\square$

Theorem 4.7   *In the one-malicious model, the algorithms $(C, (S_1, S_2))$ are an $(O(\frac{\log^2 n}{n}), \frac{2}{3})$-outsource-secure implementation of **Exp**.*

Proof. The proposed algorithm **Exp** makes 5 calls to *Rand* plus 7 modular multiplication (MM) and 3 modular inverse (MInv) in order to compute $u^a \bmod p$ (we omit other operations such as modular additions). Also, **Exp** takes $O(\log^2 n)$ or $O(1)$ MM using the EBPV generator or table-lookup method, respectively, where n is the bit-length of the a. On the other hand, it takes roughly $1.5n$ MM to compute $u^a \bmod p$ by the square-and-multiply method. Thus, the algorithms $(C, (S_1, S_2))$ are an $O(\frac{\log^2 n}{n})$-efficient implementation of **Exp**.

On the other hand, S_1 (resp. S_2) cannot distinguish the two test queries from all of the three queries that C makes. If S_1 (resp. S_2) fails during any execution of **Exp**, it will be detected with probability $\frac{2}{3}$. □

4.3.3 COMPARISON

We compare the above algorithm **Exp** [49] with Hohenberger-Lysyanskaya's algorithm in [82]. We denote by MM a modular multiplication, by MInv a modular inverse, and by Rand[Invoke] an invocation of the subroutine *Rand*. We omit other operations such as modular additions in both algorithms. Table 4.1 presents the comparison of the efficiency and the checkability between Hohenberger-Lysyanskaya's algorithm and the algorithm **Exp**.

Table 4.1: Comparison of the two algorithms

	Algorithm [84]	Algorithm Exp [49]
MM	9	7
MInv	5	3
Invoke (*Rand*)	6	5
Invoke (S_1)	4	3
Invoke (S_2)	4	3
Checkability	½	⅔

Compared with Hohenberger-Lysyanskaya's algorithm, the proposed algorithm **Exp** is superior in both efficiency and checkability. More precisely, **Exp** requires only 7 MM, 3 MInv, 5 invocation of *Rand*, and 3 invocation of S_1 and S_2 for each modular exponentiation. Note that the modular exponentiation is the most basic operation in discrete-logarithm-based cryptographic protocols, and millions of such computations may be outsourced to the server every day. Thus, our proposed algorithm can save huge computational resources for both the outsourcer C and the servers S_1 and S_2.

On the other hand, **Exp** requires only 3 invocation of S_1 and S_2 for each modular exponentiation, thus the communication overload is $6(|p| + |q|)$. However, the communication overload of algorithm [82] is $8(|p| + |q|)$ since it requires 4 invocation of S_1 and S_2.

4.4   SECURE OUTSOURCING OF SIMULTANEOUS MODULAR EXPONENTIATION

In this section, we focus on simultaneous modular exponentiations $u_1^a u_2^b \mod p$, which play an important role in many cryptographic primitives such as chameleon hashing [5, 6, 42, 44, 46, 90, 114] and trapdoor commitment [9, 80, 108]. Trivially, a simultaneous modular exponentiation can be carried out by invoking 2 modular exponentiations. This requires roughly $3n$ MM, where n is the bit-length of a and b. However, the computation cost is only $1.75n$ MM (i.e., roughly 1.17 modular exponentiation) if we use the simultaneous multiple exponentiation algorithm from Chapter 14 of [99].

Recently, Chen et al. [49] proposed the first efficient outsource-secure algorithm of simultaneous modular exponentiations **SExp** in the one-malicious model. In the following, we give an introduction for this outsourcing algorithm. Note that **SExp** also uses the same subroutine *Rand* as in Section 4.3.

4.4.1 OUTSOURCING ALGORITHM

Let p, q be two large primes and $q | p - 1$. Given two arbitrary bases $u_1, u_2 \in \mathbb{Z}_p^*$ and two arbitrary powers $a, b \in \mathbb{Z}_q^*$ such that the order of u_1 and u_2 is q. The output of **SExp** is $u_1^a u_2^b \mod p$. Both a and u are computationally blinded to U_1 and S_2.

1. C firstly runs *Rand* twice to create two blinding pairs (α, g^α) and (β, g^β). We denote $v = g^\alpha \mod p$ and $\mu = g^\beta \mod p$.

2. The first logical divisions are

$$u_1^a u_2^b = (v w_1)^a (v w_2)^b = g^\beta g^\gamma w_1^a w_2^b,$$

where $w_1 = u_1/v$, $w_2 = S_2/v$, and $\gamma = (a + b)\alpha - \beta$.

The second logical divisions are

$$u_1^a u_2^b = g^\beta g^\gamma w_1^a w_2^b = g^\beta g^\gamma w_1^k w_1^l w_2^t w_2^s,$$

where $l = a - k$ and $s = b - t$.

3. Next, C runs *Rand* to obtain three pairs (t_1, g^{t_1}), (t_2, g^{t_2}), and (t_3, g^{t_3}).

4. C queries S_1 in random order as

$S_1(t_2/t_1, g^{t_1}) \rightarrow g^{t_2}$;

$S_1(\gamma/t_3, g^{t_3}) \rightarrow g^\gamma$;

$S_1(k, w_1) \rightarrow w_1^k$;

$S_1(t, w_2) \rightarrow w_2^t$.

Similarly, C queries S_2 in random order as

$S_2(t_2/t_1, g^{t_1}) \rightarrow g^{t_2}$;

$S_2(\gamma/t_3, g^{t_3}) \rightarrow g^\gamma$;

$S_2(l, w_1) \rightarrow w_1^l$;

$S_2(s, w_2) \rightarrow w_2^s$.

5. Finally, C checks that both S_1 and S_2 produce the correct outputs, i.e., $g^{t_2} = S_1(t_2/t_1, g^{t_1}) = S_2(t_2/t_1, g^{t_1})$ and $S_1(\gamma/t_3, g^{t_3}) = S_2(\gamma/t_3, g^{t_3})$. If not, C outputs "error"; otherwise, C can compute $u_1^a u_2^b = \mu g^\gamma w_1^k w_1^l w_2^t w_2^s$.

Similar to theorem 3.1 and 3.2, we can easily prove the following theorem:

Theorem 4.8 *In the one-malicious model, the algorithms $(C, (S_1, S_2))$ are an $(O(\frac{\log^2 n}{n}), \frac{1}{2})$-outsource-secure implementation of SExp.*

4.4.2 EFFICIENCY

Note that **SExp** requires only 10 MM, 4 MInv, 5 invocation of *Rand*, and 4 invocation of S_1 and S_2 for each modular exponentiation. Therefore, the computation cost of **SExp** is much less than that of double running **Exp**. Surprisingly, it is even comparable to that of outsourcing *one* modular exponentiation [82]. Table 4.2 presents the comparison of the efficiency and the checkability between Hohenberger-Lysyanskaya's *Exp* algorithm and our proposed algorithm **SExp**.

Table 4.2: Efficiency comparison for two algorithms

	Algorithm [84]	Algorithm SExp [49]
MM	9	10
MInv	5	4
Invoke (*Rand*)	6	5
Invoke (S_1)	4	4
Invoke (S_2)	4	4
Checkability	½	½

4.5 SECURE OUTSOURCING OF BILINEAR PAIRINGS

Chevallier-Mames et al. [37] presented the first algorithm for secure delegation of elliptic-curve pairings based on an untrusted server model. Besides, the outsourcer could detect any failures with probability 1 if the server misbehaves. However, an obvious disadvantage of the algorithm is that the outsourcer should carry out some other expensive operations such as point multiplications and exponentiations. More precisely, on the one hand, we argue that these expensive operations might be too resource consuming to be carried out on a computationally limited device. On the other hand, the computation of point multiplications is even comparable to that of bilinear pairings in some scenarios [72, 116].[5] Therefore, it is meaningless if the client must perform point

---

[5]As pointed out in [72, 116], when the supersingular elliptic curve is defined over a 512-bit finite field with embedding degree 2, the computational overhead of a point multiplication is almost the same as that of a standard Tate pairing.

multiplications and exponentiations in order to outsource pairings, since this contradicts the aim of outsourcing computation.

In the following, we introduce a new secure outsourcing algorithm **Pair** for bilinear pairings in the one-malicious model [53]. A distinguishing property of the algorithm is that the (resource-constrained) client never performs any expensive operations such as point multiplications and exponentiations. Besides, in the algorithm [53], note that $\mathbb{G}_1$ and $\mathbb{G}_2$ are two cyclic additive groups of order q and $\mathbb{G}_T$ is a cyclic multiplicative cycle group of the same order. The pairing is a map $e : \mathbb{G}_1 \times \mathbb{G}_2 \to \mathbb{G}_T$. Trivially, it is no difference if we use the notations for multiplicative groups of $\mathbb{G}_1$ and $\mathbb{G}_2$.

4.5.1   OUTSOURCING ALGORITHM

The input of **Pair** is two random points $A \in \mathbb{G}_1$, $B \in \mathbb{G}_2$, and the output of **Pair** is $e(A, B)$. Note that A and B may be secret or (honest/adversarial) protected and $e(A, B)$ is always secret or protected. Moreover, both A and B are computationally blinded to S_1 and S_2. We let $S_i(\Lambda_1, \Lambda_2) \to e(\Lambda_1, \Lambda_2)$ denote that S_i takes as inputs (Λ_1, Λ_2) and outputs $e(\Lambda_1, \Lambda_2)$, where $i = 1, 2$. The proposed outsourcing algorithm **Pair** consists of the following steps:

1. To implement this functionality using S_1 and S_2, C firstly runs *Rand* to create a blinding six-tuple $(V_1, V_2, v_1 V_1, v_2 V_1, v_2 V_2, e(v_1 V_1, v_2 V_2))$. We denote $\lambda = e(v_1 V_1, v_2 V_2)$.

2. The main trick of **Pair** is to logically split A and B into random looking pieces that can be computed by S_1 and S_2. Without loss of generality, let $\alpha_1 = e(A + v_1 V_1, B + v_2 V_2)$, $\alpha_2 = e(A + V_1, v_2 V_2)$, and $\alpha_3 = e(v_1 V_1, B + V_2)$. Note that

$$\alpha_1 = e(A, B)e(A, v_2 V_2)e(v_1 V_1, B)e(v_1 V_1, v_2 V_2),$$

$$\alpha_2 = e(A, v_2 V_2)e(V_1, v_2 V_2),$$

$$\alpha_3 = e(v_1 V_1, B)e(v_1 V_1, V_2),$$

Therefore, $e(A, B) = \alpha_1 \alpha_2^{-1} \alpha_3^{-1} \lambda^{-1} e(V_1, V_2)^{v_1 + v_2}$.

3. C then runs *Rand* to obtain two new six-tuple

$$(X_1, X_2, x_1 X_1, x_2 X_1, x_2 X_2, e(x_1 X_1, x_2 X_2))$$

and

$$(Y_1, Y_2, y_1 Y_1, y_2 Y_1, y_2 Y_2, e(y_1 Y_1, y_2 Y_2)).$$

4. C queries S_1 in random order as

$$S_1(A + v_1 V_1, B + v_2 V_2) \to e(A + v_1 V_1, B + v_2 V_2) = \alpha_1;$$

$$S_1(v_1 V_1 + v_2 V_1, V_2) \to e(V_1, V_2)^{v_1 + v_2};$$

$$S_1(x_1 X_1, x_2 X_2) \rightarrow e(x_1 X_1, x_2 X_2);$$

$$S_1(y_1 Y_1, y_2 Y_2) \rightarrow e(y_1 Y_1, y_2 Y_2);$$

Similarly, C queries S_2 in random order as

$$S_2(A + V_1, v_2 V_2) \rightarrow e(A + V_1, v_2 V_2) = \alpha_2;$$

$$S_2(v_1 V_1, B + V_2) \rightarrow e(v_1 V_1, B + V_2) = \alpha_3;$$

$$S_2(x_1 X_1, x_2 X_2) \rightarrow e(x_1 X_1, x_2 X_2);$$

$$S_2(y_1 Y_1, y_2 Y_2) \rightarrow e(y_1 Y_1, y_2 Y_2);$$

5. Finally, C checks that both S_1 and S_2 produce the correct outputs, i.e., $e(x_1 X_1, x_2 X_2)$ and $e(y_1 Y_1, y_2 Y_2)$ for the test queries. If not, C outputs "error"; otherwise, C can compute $e(A, B) = \alpha_1 \alpha_2^{-1} \alpha_3^{-1} \lambda^{-1} e(V_1, V_2)^{v_1 + v_2}$.

Remark 3. Given a random point P in $\mathbb{G}_1$ (or $\mathbb{G}_2$), C can compute the inverse point $-P$ easily. Therefore, C can query $S_2(A + V_1, -v_2 V_2) \rightarrow e(A + V_1, -v_2 V_2) = \alpha_2^{-1}$ and $S_2(-v_1 V_1, B + V_2) \rightarrow e(-v_1 V_1, B + V_2) = \alpha_3^{-1}$. Similarly, we can define the outputs of *Rand* as

$$(V_1, V_2, v_1 V_1, v_2 V_1, v_2 V_2, e(v_1 V_1, v_2 V_2)^{-1}).$$

Therefore, C need not perform the inverse computation in $\mathbb{G}_T$.

4.5.2   IMPROVED OUTSOURCING ALGORITHM

Recently, Tian et al. [122] proposed a new algorithm for securely outsourcing bilinear pairings based on the two untrusted model, where the two cloud servers are both malicious while not in collusion with each other. Otherwise, we can view them as one untrusted server. On the other hand, we should emphasize that the security model in **Pair** [53] is actually one malicious version of the two untrusted program model (at most one of the two servers is malicious).

The proposed algorithm consists of the following steps:

1. To implement this functionality using S_1 and S_2, C firstly runs *Rand** twice to create two blinding six-tuple

$$(x_1 P_1, x_1 x_2^{-1} x_3 P_1, x_1^{-1} x_2 P_2, x_1^{-1} x_4 P_2, e(P_1, P_2)^{x_3 + x_4 - x_2})$$

and

$$(y_1 P_1, y_1 y_2^{-1} y_3 P_1, y_1^{-1} y_2 P_2, y_1^{-1} y_4 P_2, e(P_1, P_2)^{y_3 + y_4 - y_2}).$$

Also, C randomly selects a small integer $t \in \{1, \ldots, s\}$. Generally, s could be a 20-bit integer in the real applications.

2. The main trick of **Pair*** is also to logically split A and B into random looking pieces that can be computed by S_1 and S_2. Besides, these partial results are used to represent two different but related functions f and g of $e(A, B)$, respectively. More precisely, $f(e(A, B)) = e(A, B)$ and $g(e(A, B)) = e(A, B)^t$. If and only if the verification equation $g = f^t$ holds, C is convinced that both S_1 and S_2 output the valid results. The principle is that the probability for two untrusted servers to output two results that satisfy some unknown conditions is negligible if they do not collude with each other, while in Chen et al's algorithm **Pair**, the verification equation is the relation of two test queries (not the two functions).

3. C queries S_1 in random order as

$$S_1(A + x_1 P_1, B + x_1^{-1} x_2 P_2) \rightarrow \alpha_1;$$
$$S_1(tA + y_1 y_2^{-1} y_3 P_1, -y_1^{-1} y_2 P_2) \rightarrow \alpha_2;$$
$$S_1(-y_1 P_1, B + y_1^{-1} y_4 P_2) \rightarrow \alpha_3;$$

4. Similarly, C queries S_2 in a random order as

$$S_2(tA + y_1 P_1, B + y_1^{-1} y_2 P_2) \rightarrow \alpha_1';$$
$$S_2(A + x_1 x_2^{-1} x_3 P_1, -x_1^{-1} x_2 P_2) \rightarrow \alpha_2';$$
$$S_2(-x_1 P_1, B + x_1^{-1} x_4 P_2) \rightarrow \alpha_3';$$

5. Finally, C computes

$$\Delta = \alpha_1 \alpha_2' \alpha_3' e(P_1, P_2)^{x_3 + x_4 - x_2}$$

and

$$\Delta' = \alpha_1' \alpha_2 \alpha_3 e(P_1, P_2)^{y_3 + y_4 - y_2}.$$

If $\Delta^t = \Delta'$ and $\Delta \in \mathbb{G}_T$, C outputs Δ as the result of $e(A, B)$. Otherwise, outputs "error."

Remark 4. As pointed out in [39], it is essential to test the membership of an output, i.e., $\Delta \in \mathbb{G}_T$. The reason is that a malicious program may modify a response by multiplying an element of small orders. For some parameter sets given in [30, 113], the membership test does not need an exponentiation. A more general solution is to outsource the membership test operation. Since S_1 or S_2 knows the order q, we may use a secure public-exponent-secret-base outsourcing algorithm [134] to compute Δ^q and compare the result with $e(P_1, P_2)$ to determine whether $\Delta \in \mathbb{G}_T$.

CHAPTER 5

Secure Outsourcing of Large Database With Updates

In this chapter, we mainly focus on secure outsourcing of large database (i.e., outsourcing storage). That is, assume that a resource-constrained client would like to store a very large database on a server so that it could later retrieve a database record and update a record by assigning a new value. If the server attempts to tamper with the database, it will be detected by the client with an overwhelming probability. Besides, the computation and storage resources invested by the client must not depend on the size of the database (except for an initial setup phase). Recently, plenty of research has been done on this hot topic [84, 102, 104, 112, 127, 133].

For the case of static database, we can easily solve the problem of outsourcing storage by using message authentication codes or digital signatures. However, it is another thing if the client (frequently) performs updates on the database. As noted in [18], the main technical difficulty in this case is that the client must have a mechanism to revoke the signatures given to the server for the previous values. Otherwise, the malicious server can utilize the previous (while valid) database records and corresponding signatures to respond to the current query of the client. In order to solve this issue, the client should keep track of every change locally. However, this totally contradicts the goal of outsourcing, i.e., the client should use much fewer resources than those needed to store the database locally.

Previous research on outsourcing dynamic databases is mainly based on accumulators [56, 57, 105] and authenticated data structures [98, 107, 109, 121]. However, Benabbas, Gennaro, and Vahlis [18] pointed out that these solutions either rely on non-constant size assumptions (such as the strong Diffie-Hellman assumption) or require expensive operations (such as re-shuffling procedures) [18]. Besides, they introduced a new primitive called verifiable database (VDB) to solve the problem. They also presented the first practical VDB scheme which relies on a constant size assumption in bilinear groups of composite order. However, the scheme only supports private verifiability, that is, only the owner of the database can verify the correctness of the proofs. In some scenarios, especially in the case that the database owner is not the database user, it is essential to achieve public verifiability (i.e., anyone can verify the correctness of the proofs). Motivated by this issue, Catalano and Fiore [41] proposed an elegant solution to build VDB from vector commitment. Besides, another advantage of this construction is that it relies on standard constant-size assumption.

5.1   SECURITY DEFINITIONS

We consider the database DB as a set of tuples (x, m_x) in some appropriate domain, where x is an index and m_x is the corresponding value. Informally, a VDB scheme allows a resource-constrained client C to outsource the storage of a very large database to a server S in such a way that C can later retrieve and update the database records from S. Inherently, any attempts to tamper with the data by the dishonest S will be detected with an overwhelming probability when C queries the database. In order to achieve the confidentiality of the data record m_x, C can use a master secret key to encrypt each m_x using a symmetric encryption scheme such as AES. Trivially, given the ciphertext v_x, only C can compute the record m_x. Therefore, we only need to consider the case of encrypted database (x, v_x). This is implicitly assumed in the existing academic research.

The formal definition for verifiable databases with updates is given as follows [18, 41]:

Definition 5.1   A verifiable database scheme with updates
VDB = (**Setup, Query, Verify, Update**) consists of four algorithms defined below.

- **Setup**$(1^k, \text{DB})$: On input the security parameter k, the setup algorithm is run by the client to generate a secret key SK to be secretly stored by the client, a database encoding S that is given to the server, and a public key PK that is distributed to all users (including the client itself) for verifying the proofs.

- **Query**$(\text{PK, S}, x)$: On input an index x, the query algorithm is run by the server, and returns a pair $\tau = (v, \pi)$.

- **Verify**$(\text{PK/SK}, x, \tau)$: The public verification algorithm outputs a value v if τ is correct with respect to x, and an error $\perp$ otherwise.

- **Update**(SK, x, v'): In the update algorithm, the client firstly generates a token t'_x with the secret key SK and then sends the pair (t'_x, v') to the server. Then the server uses v' to update the database record in index x, and t'_x to update the public key PK.

There are two different kinds of verifiability for the outputs of the query algorithm, i.e., $\tau = (v, \pi)$. In the Catalano-Fiore's scheme [41], anyone can verify the validity of τ with the public key PK. Therefore, it satisfies the property of public verifiability. However, in some applications, only the client can verify the proofs generated by the server since the secret key of the client is involved in the verification. This is called private verifiability [18]. A verifiable database scheme should support both types of verifiability for various applications.

5.1.1   SECURITY REQUIREMENTS

In the following, we introduce some security requirements for a VDB scheme. The first requirement is the **security** of a VDB scheme. Intuitively, a VDB scheme is secure if a malicious server cannot convince a verifier to accept an invalid output, i.e., $v \neq v_x$ where v_x is the value of a database record in the index x. Note that v_x can be either the initial value given by the client in the setup stage or the latest value assigned by the client in the update procedure. Benabbas, Gennaro, and Vahlis [18] presented the following definition:

Definition 5.2   (**Security**) A VDB scheme is secure if for any database $DB \in [q] \times \{0, 1\}^*$, where $q = poly(k)$, and for any probabilistic polynomial time (PPT) adversary A,

$$\mathrm{Adv}_A(\mathsf{VDB}, DB, k) \leq \mathrm{negl}(k),$$

where $\mathrm{Adv}_A(\mathsf{VDB}, DB, k) = \Pr[\mathbf{Exp}_A^{\mathsf{VDB}}(DB, k) = 1]$ is defined as the advantage of A in the experiment as follows:

$$
\begin{aligned}
&\text{Experiment } \mathbf{Exp}_A^{\mathsf{VDB}}[DB, k] \\
&\quad (\mathsf{PK}, \mathsf{SK}) \leftarrow Setup(DB, k); \\
&\quad \text{For } i = 1, \ldots, l = poly(k); \\
&\qquad \textbf{Verify query}: \\
&\qquad\quad (x_i, \tau_i) \leftarrow A(\mathsf{PK}, t_1', \ldots, t_{i-1}'); \\
&\qquad\quad v_i \leftarrow Verify(\mathsf{PK/SK}, x_i, \tau_i); \\
&\qquad \textbf{Update query}: \\
&\qquad\quad (x_i, v_{x_i}^{(i)}) \leftarrow A(\mathsf{PK}, t_1', \ldots, t_{i-1}'); \\
&\qquad\quad t_i' \leftarrow Update(\mathsf{SK}, x_i, v_{x_i}^{(i)}); \\
&\quad (\hat{x}, \hat{\tau}) \leftarrow A(\mathsf{PK}, t_1', \ldots, t_l'); \\
&\quad \hat{v} \leftarrow Verify(\mathsf{PK/SK}, \hat{x}, \hat{\tau}) \\
&\qquad \text{If } \hat{v} \neq \perp \text{ and } \hat{v} \neq v_{\hat{x}}^{(l)}, \text{output 1; else output 0.}
\end{aligned}
$$

In the above experiment, after every update query, we implicitly assign $\mathsf{PK} \leftarrow \mathsf{PK}_i$. Note that this property of security is similar to that of soundness in zero-knowledge proof.

The second requirement is the **correctness** of a VDB scheme. That is, the value and proof generated by the honest server can always be verified successfully and accepted by the client (the honest server results in valid results and proof). This is similar to the property of completeness in zero-knowledge proof.

Definition 5.3   (**Correctness**) A VDB scheme is correct if for any database $DB \in [q] \times \{0, 1\}^*$, where $q = poly(k)$, and for any valid pair $\tau = (v, \pi)$ generated by an honest server, the output of the verification algorithm is always the value v.

The third requirement is the **efficiency** of a VDB scheme. That is, the client in the verifiable database scheme should not be involved in much expensive computation and storage (except for an initial pre-processing phase).[6]

Definition 5.4 (**Efficiency**) A VDB scheme is efficient if for any database $DB \in [q] \times \{0, 1\}^*$, where $q = poly(k)$, the computation and storage resources invested by the client must be independent of q.

The last requirement is the **accountability** for a VDB scheme. That is, after the client has detected the tampering of dishonest server, he should provide some evidence to convince a judge of the facts.

Definition 5.5 (**Accountability**) A VDB scheme is accountable if for any database $DB \in [q] \times \{0, 1\}^*$, where $q = poly(k)$, the client can provide a proof if the dishonest server has tampered with the database.

5.1.2   FORWARD AUTOMATIC/BACKWARD SUBSTITUTION UPDATE ATTACK

In the following, we consider two attacks on VDB schemes. Basically, both of them violate the **Security** and **Accountability** properties of VDB in the above definition.

The first attack is that an adversary A (i.e., the malicious server S) can perform the **Update** algorithm in the same way as the client C. Specifically, S firstly retrieves the current record v_x and then computes the token t_x^* (if the computation does not need any secret knowledge of C). Finally, S updates the corresponding database record with any new value v_x^*, and the public key PK* with t_x^*. Trivially, S can generate a valid proof for any query based on PK*. Besides, this *forward* updated public key PK* and the real one PK' are totally computationally indistinguishable from a viewpoint of any third party. Therefore, when a dispute occurs, a judge cannot deduce that S is dishonest. We define this kind of adversary as *Forward Automatic Update* (FAU) attacker.

The second attack on VDB schemes is not explicitly stated in previous literature. We call it *Backward Substitution Update* (BSU) attack. That is, the dishonest S can utilize the previous (while valid) public key and the corresponding database to substitute the current ones (trivially, this can also be viewed as an update). We argue that S in VDB has the ability to update the public key freely. If this case happens, the effort of the later update by C is no longer meaningful. Furthermore, if C did not store the public key locally, it is difficult for him to distinguish the past public key from the latest one. On the other hand, even if C has stored the latest public key, it seems still to be difficult for him to prove the fact that the stored public key is the latest one.

---

[6]In some scenarios, the client is allowed to invest a one-time expensive computational effort. This is known as the amortized model of outsourcing computations [74].

5.2   VDB CONSTRUCTION FROM DELEGATING POLYNOMIAL FUNCTIONS

In this section, we introduce Benabbas-Gennaro-Vahlis VDB scheme from delegating high degree polynomial functions. This is the first efficient VDB construction that relies on a "constant-size" assumption (i.e., the subgroup member assumption).

5.2.1   DELEGATING OF POLYNOMIAL FUNCTIONS

Given a polynomial $P(x) = \sum_{i=0}^{d} c_i x^i$, where $c_i \in \mathbb{Z}_p$. The aim is to compute $y = P(u)$. The outsourcing protocol between C and S is given as follows:

Let $R(x) = \sum_{i=0}^{d} r_i x^i$, where $r_i \in \mathbb{Z}_p$. C computes and then shares with S a vector $\mathbf{t}$ of the group elements with the form $g^{ac_i + r_i}$, where $a \in_R \mathbb{Z}_p$ is a random value which is only known by C. Given the query u, S returns $y = P(u)$ and $t = g^{aP(u)+R(u)}$. C accepts y iff $t = g^{ay+R(u)}$.

The crucial point is how C can compute $R(u)$ efficiently. If $R(x)$ is a random polynomial, then the computational overload of $R(u)$ is the same as that of $P(u)$. The trick is that we can use an algebraic PRF that has a closed form efficient computation for polynomials such that $g^{r_i} = F_K(i)$, where K is a secret key of F. In this case, the security of the construction is not compromised, while the closed form efficiency of F will allow C to verify the result efficiently.

In the following, we present a concrete protocol for delegating polynomials with a certain algebraic PRF $F_K(i) = g^{k_0 k_1^i}$ (note that we could use any other algebraic PRF). Define $R(x) = \sum_{i=0}^{d} r_i x^i = \sum_{i=0}^{d} k_0 k_1^i x^i$. Then, C can compute $R(u)$ efficiently for any u.

1. **KeyGen**: Given a security parameter k and the target function is $P(x) = \sum_{i=0}^{d} c_i x^i$. Let $\mathbb{G}$ be the range group of F_K, and g be a generator of $\mathbb{G}$. Define $g_i = F_K(i) = g^{k_0 k_1^i}$. Choose a random $a \in_R \mathbb{Z}_p$ and compute $T = (t_0, ..., t_d) = (g_0 g^{ac_0}, ..., g_d g^{ac_d})$. Output $PK = (T, P(x))$ and $SK = (K, a) = (k_0, k_1, a)$.

2. **ProbGen**: Given the input u, output $\sigma_u = u$ and $\tau_u = u$.

3. **Compute**: Given the public key PK and the encoded input σ_u, S computes $h(u) = (1, u, \ldots, u^d) \in \mathbb{Z}_p^{d+1}$, $y = \sum_{i=0}^{d} c_i u^i$, and $t = \prod_{i=0}^{d} t_i^{u^i}$. Output $\sigma_u = (y, t)$.

4. **Verify**: C computes $z = \text{CFEval}_h(u, K)$ and accepts y iff $t = z g^{ay}$.

The correctness of the protocol is due to the fact below:

$$z = \text{CFEval}_h(u, K) = \prod_{i=0}^{d} [F_K(i)]^{u^i} = \prod_{i=0}^{d} g^{k_0 k_1^i u^i} = \prod_{i=0}^{d} g^{r_i u^i} = g^{R(u)}$$

Note that this protocol does not ensure the privacy of the polynomials. Though the issue could be solved by using an additively homomorphic encryption scheme, it still does not protect the privacy of input u.

5.2.2   BENABBAS-GENNARO-VAHLIS VDB CONSTRUCTION

In this section, we introduce Benabbas-Gennaro-Vahlis's VDB scheme in the setting of bilinear groups of composite order. The scheme consists of the following algorithms:

- **Setup:** The setup algorithm takes as input a security parameter n and an encrypted database DB with the form of $(i, v_i) \in [q] \times \mathbb{Z}_{n-1}$. Trivially, we could use a hash function $H : \{0, 1\}^* \to \mathbb{Z}_{n-1}$ to proceed a very large data record v_i. It then generates the bilinear pairing groups $\mathbb{G}, \mathbb{G}_T$ of order $N = p_1 p_2$, where p_1, p_2 are primes in the range $[2^{n-1}, 2^n - 1]$, and a pairing $e : \mathbb{G} \times \mathbb{G} \to \mathbb{G}_T$. Let $\mathbb{G}_1$ and $\mathbb{G}_2$ be subgroups of $\mathbb{G}$ of orders p and q, respectively. Choose two PRF keys k_1, k_2 randomly, and choose randomly:

$$g_1, h_1 \in_R \mathbb{G}_1, g_2, h_2, u_2 \in_R \mathbb{G}_2, a, b \in_R \mathbb{Z}_N$$

  For each $i \in \{1, \ldots, q\}$, set $r_i = F_{k_1}(i), w_i = F_{k_2}(i, 1)$, and $s_i = 1$. Define

$$t_i = g_1^{r_i + a v_i + b s_i} g_2^{w_i}, w = \sum_{i=1}^q w_i, T_w \leftarrow e(g_2, u_2)^w.$$

  Set $\hat{t_0} = u_2$ and $\hat{t_1} = h_1 h_2$. The public key is $PK = ((\hat{t_0}, \hat{t_1}, s_1, t_1, \ldots, s_q, t_q), \text{DB})$. The private key is $SK = (a, T_w, k_1, k_2)$.

- **Query:** The query processing algorithm takes as input the public key PK and an index query $x \in \{1, \cdots, q\}$, and then computes

$$T = e(t_x, \hat{t_1}) \cdot e\left(\prod_{i=1, i \neq x}^q t_i, \hat{t_0} \right).$$

  Output $(T, y = v_x, s_x)$.

- **Verify:** The verification algorithm takes as input a private key SK, a query x, and (T, y, s_x). The verifier then computes $r_x = F_{k_1}(x), w_x = F_{k_2}(x, s_x)$ and checks

$$T \stackrel{?}{=} T_w \cdot e(g_1^{r_x + a \cdot y + b \cdot s_x} g_2, h_1 u_2^{-w_x} h_2^{w_x})$$

  If the equality holds, the verifier outputs 1. Otherwise, outputs $\perp$.

- **Update:** The update algorithm takes as input a pair $(x, y') \in [m] \times \mathbb{Z}_{n-1}$. C firstly submits x as a query to S, and verifies the validity of triple (T, y, s_x). Then sets

$$w'_x = F_{k_2}(x, s_x + 1) - F_{k_2}(x, s_x), T_w \leftarrow T_w \cdot e(g_2^{w'_x}, u_2), \text{ and } t'_x \leftarrow g_1^{a(y'-y)+b} g_2^{w'_x}.$$

S is then given t_x', and updates the public key by setting $t_x \leftarrow t_x \cdot t_x'$ and $s_x \leftarrow s_x + 1$.

The correctness of the scheme follows from properties of bilinear maps over composite order groups (that is, for any $u \in \mathbb{G}_1$ and $v \in \mathbb{G}_2$, we have $e(u, v) = 1_{\mathbb{G}_T}$):

$$T = e(t_x, \hat{t}_1)e(\prod_{i \neq x} t_i, \hat{t}_0) = e(g_1^{r_x + av_x + bs_x} g_2^{w_x}, h_1 h_2) \prod_{i \neq x} e(g_1^{r_i + av_i + bs_i} g_2^{w_i}, u_2)$$

$$= e(g_1^{r_x + av_x + bs_x} g_2, h_1 u_2^{-w_x} h_2^{w_x}) \prod_i e(g_1^{r_i + av_i + bs_i} g_2^{w_i}, u_2)$$

$$= e(g_1^{r_x + av_x + bs_x} g_2, h_1 u_2^{-w_x} h_2^{w_x}) \cdot T_w$$

Note that delegating a polynomial is used as a building block in the above construction. The polynomial is defined as $P(x) = v_x$ for all $1 \leq x \leq q$. Nevertheless, S actually did not compute the value of $P(x)$ for a query index x. That is the reason why VDB is not outsourcing computation but storage. Besides, C can reconstruct and verify the proof T by using a PRF F with closed form efficiency.

In order to prevent the BSU attack, S should compute a signature on the tuples (i, T_i), where T_i is the latest counter for index i. C should store the tuples together with the signature locally by himself and it is meaningless to store these values in the S side.

5.3   VDB FRAMEWORK BASED ON VECTOR COMMITMENT

In 2013, Catalano and Fiore presented the second efficient construction for general VDB framework using the primitive of vector commitment [41]. The elegant construction is based on the standard CDH assumption in bilinear groups. Besides, compared with the first efficient VDB construction, it can support both public verifiability and private verifiability.

In this section, we first give an overview of their VDB general framework and then present a security weakness of the construction [47].

5.3.1   THE GENERAL FRAMEWORK

The main idea of Catalano-Fiore's VDB framework is as follows: Let C be the vector commitment on the database. Given a query on index x by the client C, the server S provides the value v_x and the opening of commitment as a proof that v_x has not been tampered with. During the update phase, C computes a new ciphertext v_x' and a token t_x' and then sends them to S. Finally, S updates the database and the corresponding public key with the pair (t_x', v_x'). Formally, the framework consists of the following algorithms:

- **Setup**(1^k, DB): Let the database be DB $= (i, v_i)$ for $1 \leq i \leq q$. Run the key generation algorithm of vector commitment to obtain the public parameters PP $\leftarrow$ VC.KeyGen($1^k, q$).

Run the committing algorithm to compute the commitment and auxiliary information $(C, \text{aux}) \leftarrow \text{VC.Com}_{\text{PP}}(v_1, \cdots, v_q)$. Define $\text{PK} = (\text{PP}, C)$ as the public key of VDB scheme, $S = (\text{PP}, \text{aux}, \text{DB})$ as the database encoding, and $\text{SK} = /$ as the secret key of C.

- **Query**(PK, S, x): On input an index x, S firstly runs the opening algorithm to compute $\pi_x \leftarrow \text{VC.Open}_{\text{PP}}(v_x, x, \text{aux})$ and then returns $\tau = (v_x, \pi_x)$.

- **Verify**(PK, x, τ): Parse the proofs $\tau = (v_x, \pi_x)$. If $\text{VC.Ver}_{\text{PP}}(C, x, v_x, \pi_x) = 1$, then return v_x. Otherwise, return an error $\perp$.

- **Update**(SK, x, v'): To update the record of index x, C firstly retrieves the current record v_x from S. That is, C obtains $\tau \leftarrow \textbf{Query}(\text{PK}, S, x)$ from S and checks that **Verify**$(\text{PK}, x, \tau) = v_x \neq \perp$. Also, C computes $(C', U) \leftarrow \text{VC.Update}_{\text{PP}}(C, v_x, x, v'_x)$ and outputs $\text{PK}' = (\text{PP}, C')$ and $t'_x = (\text{PK}', v'_x, U)$. Then S uses v'_x to update the database record of index x, PK' to update the public key, and U to update the auxiliary information.

5.3.2   SECURITY ANALYSIS

In this section, we present a security analysis of Catalano-Fiore's VDB general framework and show the framework suffers from both the FAU and BSU attack [47].

Firstly, we argue that Catalano-Fiore's VDB framework suffers from the FAU attack. The main reason is that the secret key in Catalano-Fiore's VDB construction is assumed to be empty, i.e., $\text{SK} = /$. As a result, anyone can verify the validity of output τ and thus the construction supports the public verifiability. However, this also allows the adversary A to update the database in an indistinguishable manner as the client since no secret information is required in the update algorithm.[7] Besides, it is more difficult for the third party to detect the FAU attack than the client. Therefore, VDB schemes that support the public verifiability are more vulnerable to the FAU attack in the real-world applications. In the following, we present the formal proof that Catalano-Fiore's framework violates the **security** definition of VDB.

Theorem 5.6   *Catalano-Fiore's VDB framework does not satisfy the property of security.*

Proof.   A VDB scheme does not satisfy the property of security means that the adversary A (i.e., the dishonest server) can successfully simulate the experiment $\textbf{Exp}_A^{\text{VDB}}[\text{DB}, k]$ and win the game with a non-negligible probability. In Catalano-Fiore's VDB framework, the secret key is assumed to be empty, i.e., $\text{SK} = \perp$. Therefore, the adversary A can perform the algorithm **Update** freely. Our main trick is that we require A to perform an additional round of **Update** after finishing l rounds of **Update** queries of the client. However, in the last round of **Update**, A also plays the role of client. More precisely, the simulated experiment $\textbf{Exp}'^{\text{VDB}}_A[\text{DB}, k]$ is defined as follows:

---

[7]Note that the construction [18] only supports the private verifiability since the (non-empty) secret key SK is involved in the verification. Besides, SK is also involved in the update algorithm and hence only the client can update the database.

Experiment $\mathbf{Exp}'^{VDB}_A[DB, k]$
  $(PK, \perp) \leftarrow \mathbf{Setup}(DB, k)$;
  For $i = 1, \ldots, l + 1$; where $l = poly(k)$;
    Verify query :
      $(x_i, \tau_i) \leftarrow A(PK, t'_1, \ldots, t'_{i-1})$;
      $v_i \leftarrow \mathbf{Verify}(PK/\perp, x_i, \tau_i)$;
    Update query :
      $(x_i, v^{(i)}_{x_i}) \leftarrow A(PK, t'_1, \ldots, t'_{i-1})$;
      $t'_i \leftarrow \mathbf{Update}(\perp, x_i, v^{(i)}_{x_i})$;
  $(\hat{x}, \hat{\tau}) \leftarrow A(PK, t'_1, \ldots, t'_{l+1})$;
  $\hat{v} \leftarrow \mathbf{Verify}(PK/\perp, \hat{x}, \hat{\tau})$

Since we implicitly assign $PK \leftarrow PK_i$ after every update query in the experiment, the final public key $PK = PK_{l+1}$. Then, let $\hat{v} = v^{(l+1)}_{\hat{x}}$. Trivially, $\hat{v} \neq \perp$ and $\hat{v} \neq v^{(l)}_{\hat{x}}$. This violates the **security** definition of the VDB scheme. $\qquad\square$

Secondly, Catalano-Fiore's framework also suffers from the BSU attack since the verification only requires the public key stored by the server. Besides, it certainly does not satisfy the property of accountability. Fortunately, we could provide a straightforward effective solution to the BSU attack. The trick is as follows: we still need a counter T in the public key to denote the number of updates. The difference is that the server computes a signature σ on the latest counter T_l and the identity ID_c of the client. Given a past public key with the counter T_p, the client provides the pair (σ, T_l) to the judge as a proof. If σ is valid and $T_p < T_l$, the judge claims that the server is dishonest. Trivially, the storage workload of the client is only the latest pair (σ, T_l) (not all signatures for every counters). Therefore, we will not consider the BSU attack anymore in the remainder of this book.

Remark 5. It seems that there are two naive approaches against FAU attack for Catalano-Fiore's VDB framework. The first solution is that we can require the server to compute a signature on the (updated) public key. However, we argue that this solution does not work since the dishonest server is an inherent FAU attacker in Catalano-Fiore's VDB framework (the server has the ability to compute the signature on any public key). The second one is that the client computes a signature on the (updated) public key. Obviously, the server cannot forge the client's signature. However, it requires that the client must have a mechanism to revoke the previous signatures (surprisingly, it reverted to the same problem of VDB). Therefore, neither of the two approaches can solve the security issue of Catalano-Fiore's constructions.

Remark 6. Note that Benabbas-Gennaro-Vahlis's scheme [18] does not suffer from BSU attack since the secret key of the client is updated each time. Without loss of generality, assume that the latest secret key of the client is SK_l. When the dishonest server presents a previous public key PK_p including a counter T_p and the corresponding database DB_p, it is trivial that the output of query algorithm by the server cannot pass the verification with the secret key SK_l. As a result, the tampering will be detected by the client. However, this cannot be viewed as a proof even if the client presents his secret key to a judge. The reason is that a malicious client also has the ability to frame an honest server. That is, the malicious client can present a random value as the secret key to invalidate the verification on the output of an honest server. Thus, the judge cannot deduce who is dishonest when a dispute occurred. In this sense, we argue that Benabbas-Gennaro-Vahlis's scheme does not satisfy the property of accountability (this also indicates that accountability is a stronger notion than security). In order to achieve the accountability, the client should store the latest counter and the corresponding signature as we mentioned in the above solution to the BSU attack (we argue again that it is not sufficient only to store these values in the server's side as in [18]).

5.4　VDB FRAMEWORK FROM BINDING VECTOR COMMITMENT

In this section, we introduce Chen et al's new VDB scheme [47], which is not only public verifiable but also secure under the FAU attack. The main trick is as follows.

As stated above, the main reason that Catalano-Fiore's framework suffers from the FAU attack is that the secret key SK of the client is not involved in the computation and update of the public key PK (actually, SK is assumed to be $\perp$). This will enable the adversary (especially the dishonest server) to update PK freely. Note that $PK = (PP, C')$ and the public parameters PP of vector commitment is never updated. That is, the public parameters are generated and published by a trusted party [67]. Thus, the server can update the vector commitment C' at its own will and this equals to update the databases. We argue that it is meaningless if we add a signature of the server on C' to PK since the server can compute such a signature on any message. On the other hand, if we use SK to compute the updated public key PK (more precisely, the commitment C') just as in the scheme [18], the proposed VDB scheme might no longer support the property of public verifiability. The main reason is that the secret key SK might be also involved in the verification of C and the corresponding proofs (i.e., the openings of C). That is, only the client with SK can verify the validity of the proofs. Therefore, it seems to be contradictory to construct a VDB scheme that is public verifiable and secure under the FAU attack simultaneously.

We utilize the idea of *commitment binding* to solve this problem. That is, the client uses the secret key SK to compute a signature on some binding information which will be explained later. Also, the signature is used to compute the updated commitment C'. Since the signature is different for each updating, the server cannot compute a new C' without the cooperation of client. Also, we emphasize that the secret key SK is never used in the verification algorithm, but only used in the update algorithm.

The binding information consists of the last public key C_{T-1} (a commitment value), the commitment $C^{(T)}$ on the current database vector, and the current counter T. Assume that the signature of client on binding information is $H_T = \text{SIGN}_{sk}(C_{T-1}, C^{(T)}, T)$, then the current public key $C_T = H_T C^{(T)}$. So, the solution binds the commitment C_T to the 3-tuple $(C_{T-1}, C^{(T)}, T)$ in a recursion manner as shown in Fig. 5.1. As a result, the adversary that includes the server cannot update the database and public key freely.

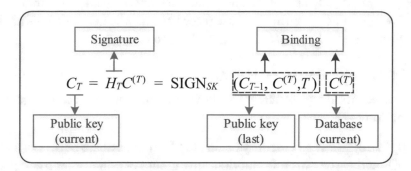

Figure 5.1: Commitment binding.

Chen et al.'s new proposed VDB framework is given as follows.

- **Setup**(1^k, DB): Let the database be DB $= (i, v_i)$ for $1 \leq i \leq q$. Let VC be any secure vector commitment scheme. Run the key generation algorithm of vector commitment to obtain the public parameters PP $\leftarrow$ VC.KeyGen($1^k, q$). Run the committing algorithm to compute the commitment and auxiliary information $(C_R, \text{aux}) \leftarrow$ VC.Com$_{PP}(v_1, \cdots, v_q)$. Let (sk, pk) be the secret/public key pair of the client C. Let SIGN be a provably secure digital signature scheme. Let T be a counter with the initial value 0. Let $C^{(T)} = $ VC.Com$_{PP}(v_1^{(T)}, \cdots, v_q^{(T)})$ be the commitment on the latest database vector after the original database DB has been updated T times. Trivially, $C^{(0)} = C_R$. Specially, let $C_{-1} = C_R$. The client C computes and sends the signature $H_0 = $ SIGN$_{sk}(C_{-1}, C^{(0)}, 0)$ to the server S. If H_0 is valid, then S computes $C_0 = H_0 C^{(0)}$. Also, S adds the information of $\Sigma_0 = (H_0, C_{-1}, C^{(0)}, 0)$ to aux.

  Set PK $= (PP, pk, C_R, C_0)$ as the public key of the VDB scheme, S $= (PP, \text{aux}, DB)$ as the database encoding, and SK $= sk$ as the secret key of C.

- **Query**(PK, S, x): Assume that the current public key PK $= (PP, pk, C_R, C_T)$. On input an index x, S runs the opening algorithm to compute $\pi_x \leftarrow$ VC.Open$_{PP}(v_x, x, \text{aux})$ and returns $\tau = (v_x, \pi_x, \Sigma_T)$, where $\Sigma_T = (H_T, C_{T-1}, C^{(T)}, T)$.

- **Verify**(PK, x, τ): Parse $\tau = (v_x, \pi_x, \Sigma_T)$. If Ver$_{pk}(\Sigma_T) = 1$ (this means that H_T is a valid signature of C on message $(C_{T-1}, C^{(T)}, T)$) and VC.Ver$_{PP}(C_T, H_T, x, v_x, \pi_x) = 1$, then return v_x. Otherwise, return an error $\perp$.

- **Update**(SK, x, v_x'): To update the record of index x, C firstly retrieves the current record v_x from S as in the above **Verify** algorithm. That is, C firstly obtains $\tau \leftarrow$ **Query**(PK, S, x)

from S and then checks that $\textbf{Verify}(\text{PK}, x, \tau) = v_x \neq \bot$. Set $T \leftarrow T + 1$, C firstly computes $\text{C}^{(T)} = \text{VC.Com}_{\text{PP}}(v_1^{(T)}, \cdots, v_q^{(T)})$ and $t_x' = H_T = \text{Sign}_{sk}(\text{C}_{T-1}, \text{C}^{(T)}, T)$, and then sends (t_x', v_x') to S. If t_x' is valid, then S computes $\text{C}_T = H_T \text{C}^{(T)}$ and updates the public key $\text{PK} = (\text{PP}, pk, \text{C}_R, \text{C}_T)$ (note that only the value of C_T needs to be updated). Also, S uses the value of v_x' to update the database record of index x, i.e., $\text{DB}(x) \leftarrow v_x'$. Finally, S adds the information of $\Sigma_T = (H_T, \text{C}_{T-1}, \text{C}^{(T)}, T)$ to aux in S.

5.4.1   A CONCRETE VDB SCHEME

In this section, we introduce a concrete VDB scheme from the vector commitments based on the CDH assumption [47].

- **Setup**(1^k, DB): Let k be a security parameter. Let the database be $\text{DB} = (x, v_x)$ for $1 \leq x \leq q$. Let $\mathbb{G}_1$ and $\mathbb{G}_2$ be two cyclic multiplicative groups of prime order p equipped with a bilinear pairing $e : \mathbb{G}_1 \times \mathbb{G}_1 \rightarrow \mathbb{G}_2$. Let g be a generator of $\mathbb{G}_1$. Let $\mathcal{H} : \mathbb{G}_1 \times \mathbb{G}_1 \times \{0, 1\}^* \rightarrow \mathbb{G}_1$ be a cryptographic hash function. Randomly choose q elements $z_i \in_R \mathbb{Z}_p$ and compute $h_i = g^{z_i}, h_{i,j} = g^{z_i z_j}$, where $1 \leq i, j \leq q$ and $i \neq j$.

  Set $\text{PP} = (p, q, \mathbb{G}_1, \mathbb{G}_2, \mathcal{H}, e, g, \{h_i\}_{1 \leq i \leq q}, \{h_{i,j}\}_{1 \leq i, j \leq q, i \neq j})$, and the message space $\mathcal{M} = \mathbb{Z}_p$. C randomly selects an element $y \in_R \mathbb{Z}_p$ and then computes $Y = g^y$.

  Let $\text{C}_R = \prod_{i=1}^q h_i^{v_i}$ be the root commitment on the database vector $(v_1, v_2, \cdots, v_q)$. Let T be a counter with the initial value 0. Let $\text{C}^{(T)}$ be the commitment on the latest database vector after the original database DB has been updated T times. Trivially, $\text{C}^{(0)} = \text{C}_R$. Specially, let $\text{C}_{-1} = \text{C}_R$. C computes and sends $H_0 = \mathcal{H}(\text{C}_{-1}, \text{C}^{(0)}, 0)^y$ to S. If the equation $e(H_0, g) = e(\mathcal{H}(\text{C}_{-1}, \text{C}^{(0)}, 0), Y)$ holds (that means H_0 is a valid signature of C), then S computes $\text{C}_0 = H_0 \text{C}^{(0)}$. Also, S adds the information of $(H_0, \text{C}_{-1}, \text{C}^{(0)}, 0)$ to aux.

  Set $\text{PK} = (\text{PP}, Y, \text{C}_R, \text{C}_0)$, $\text{S} = (\text{PP}, \text{aux}, \text{DB})$ and $\text{SK} = y$.

- **Query**(PK, S, x): Assume that the current public key $\text{PK} = (\text{PP}, Y, \text{C}_R, \text{C}_T)$. Given a query index x, S computes $\pi_x^{(T)} = \prod_{1 \leq j \leq q, j \neq x} h_{x,j}^{v_j^{(T)}}$ and returns the proofs

$$\tau = (v_x^{(T)}, \pi_x^{(T)}, H_T, \text{C}_{T-1}, \text{C}^{(T)}, T).$$

- **Verify**(PK, x, τ): Parse the proofs $\tau = (v_x^{(T)}, \pi_x^{(T)}, H_T, \text{C}_{T-1}, \text{C}^{(T)}, T)$. Then anyone (including the client) can verify the validity of the proofs τ by checking whether the following two equations $e(H_T, g) = e(\mathcal{H}(\text{C}_{T-1}, \text{C}^{(T)}, T), Y)$ and $e(\text{C}_T / H_T h_x^{v_x^{(T)}}, h_x) = e(\pi_x^{(T)}, g)$ hold.[8] If the proofs τ is valid, the verifier accepts it and outputs $v_x^{(T)}$. Otherwise, outputs an error $\bot$.

---

[8] If the verifier is client, then he needs only to check whether $H_T = \mathcal{H}(\text{C}_{T-1}, \text{C}^{(T)}, T)^y$ holds in order to decrease the computation overload.

- **Update**(SK, x, v'_x): To update the record of index x, C firstly retrieves the current record v_x from S. That is, C obtains $\tau \leftarrow$ **Query**($\mathsf{PK}, \mathsf{S}, x$) from S and checks that **Verify**(PK, x, τ) = $v_x \neq \perp$.

  Set $T \leftarrow T + 1$, C firstly computes $C^{(T)} = \frac{C_{T-1}}{H_{T-1}} h_x^{v'_x - v_x}$ and $t'_x = H_T = \mathcal{H}(C_{T-1}, C^{(T)}, T)^y$, and then sends (t'_x, v'_x) to S. If t'_x is valid, then S computes $C_T = H_T C^{(T)}$ and updates the public key with $\mathsf{PK} = (\mathsf{PP}, Y, C_R, C_T)$. Also, S uses the value of v'_x to update the database record of index x, i.e., $\mathsf{DB}(x) \leftarrow v'_x$. Finally, S adds the information of $(t'_x = H_T, C_{T-1}, C^{(T)}, T)$ to aux in S.

5.4.2   SECURITY ANALYSIS OF THE VDB SCHEME

In this section, we present the security analysis of the above VDB scheme.

Theorem 5.7   *The proposed VDB scheme achieves the property of security.*

Proof. Similar to [41], we can prove the theorem by contradiction. Assume there exists a polynomial-time adversary A that has a non-negligible advantage ϵ in the experiment $\mathbf{Exp}_A^{\mathsf{VDB}}[\mathsf{DB}, k]$ for some initial database DB, then we can use A to build an efficient algorithm B to break the Squ-CDH assumption. That is, B takes as input a tuple (g, g^a) and outputs g^{a^2}.

First, B randomly chooses an element $x^* \in_R \mathbb{Z}_q$ as a guess for the index x^* on which A succeeds in the experiment $\mathbf{Exp}_A^{\mathsf{VDB}}[\mathsf{DB}, k]$. Then B randomly chooses $z_i \in_R \mathbb{Z}_p$ and computes $h_i = g^{z_i}$ all $1 \leq i \neq x^* \leq q$. Let $h_{x^*} = g^a$. Besides, B computes:

$h_{i,j} = g^{z_i z_j}$ for all $1 \leq i \neq j \leq q$ and $i, j \neq x^*$;

$h_{i,x^*} = h_{x^*,i} = (g^a)^{z_i}$ for all $1 \leq i \leq q$ and $i \neq x^*$.

Set $\mathsf{PP} = (p, q, \mathbb{G}_1, \mathbb{G}_2, \mathcal{H}, e, g, \{h_i\}, \{h_{i,j}\})$, where $1 \leq i \neq j \leq q$. Then B randomly selects an element $y \in_R \mathbb{Z}_p$ and computes $Y = g^y$. Given a database DB, B computes the commitment $C_R = \prod_{i=1}^q h_i^{v_i}$. Also, B computes $H_0 = \mathcal{H}(C_R, C_R, 0)^y$ and $C_0 = H_0 C_R$. Define $\mathsf{PK} = (\mathsf{PP}, Y, C_R, C_0)$, $\mathsf{S} = (\mathsf{PP}, \text{aux}, \mathsf{DB})$ and $\mathsf{SK} = y$. B sends PK to A. Note that PK and S are perfectly distributed as the real ones.

To answer the verify and update queries of A in the experiment, B just simply runs the real Query($\mathsf{PK}, \mathsf{S}, x$) and Update($\mathsf{SK}, x, v'_x$) algorithms and responds with the same value. Note that the Update(SK, x, v'_x) algorithm requires the secret key y of B, and A cannot perform this algorithm without the help of B. Therefore, the FAU attack is no longer successful in the experiment $\mathbf{Exp}'^{\mathsf{VDB}}_A[\mathsf{DB}, k]$.

Suppose that $(\hat{x}, \hat{\tau})$ be the tuple returned by A at the end of the experiment, where $\hat{\tau} = (\hat{v}, \hat{\pi}, \Sigma_l)$. Besides, note that if A wins with a non-negligible advantage ϵ in the experiment, then we have $\hat{v} \neq \perp$, $\hat{v} \neq v_{\hat{x}}^{(l)}$ and $e(C^{(l)}, h_{\hat{x}}) = e(h_{\hat{x}}^{v_{\hat{x}}^{(l)}}, h_{\hat{x}}) e(\pi_{\hat{x}}^{(l)}, g) = e(h_{\hat{x}}^{\hat{v}}, h_{\hat{x}}) e(\hat{\pi}, g)$.

If $\hat{x} \neq x^*$, B aborts the simulation and fails. Otherwise, we have $h_{\hat{x}} = g^a$. Trivially, B can compute

$$g^{a^2} = (\hat{\pi}/\pi_{\hat{x}}^{(l)})^{(v_{\hat{x}}^{(l)} - \hat{v})^{-1}}.$$

The success probability of B is ϵ/q. $\qquad\square$

Theorem 5.8 *The proposed VDB scheme achieves the property of correctness.*

Proof. If the server is assumed to be honest in the VDB scheme, then the proofs $\tau = (v_x^{(T)}, \pi_x^{(T)}, H_T, C_{T-1}, C^{(T)}, T)$, where $\pi_x^{(T)} = \prod_{1 \leq j \leq q, j \neq x} h_{x,j}^{v_j^{(T)}}$. Firstly, note that $H_T = \mathcal{H}(C_{T-1}, C^{(T)}, T)^y$, therefore we have $e(H_T, g) = e(\mathcal{H}(C_{T-1}, C^{(T)}, T), Y)$. Secondly, due to $C_T/H_T h_x^{v_x^{(T)}} = C^{(T)}/h_x^{v_x^{(T)}} = \prod_{1 \leq j \leq q, j \neq x} h_j^{v_j^{(T)}}$, we have $e(C_T/H_T h_x^{v_x^{(T)}}, h_x) = e(\pi_x^{(T)}, g)$. Hence, the output of the verification algorithm is always the value $v_x^{(T)}$. $\qquad\square$

Theorem 5.9 *The proposed VDB scheme achieves the property of efficiency.*

Proof. It is trivial that the computational resources invested by the client in the VDB scheme is independent of q (except for a one-time **Setup** phase). $\qquad\square$

Theorem 5.10 *The proposed VDB scheme achieves the property of accountability.*

Proof. Given the proofs τ with the counter T, the client firstly compares it with the latest counter T_c he stored. If $T < T_c$, then the client sends the corresponding signature σ on T_c to the judge as the proof. Otherwise, he sends τ to the judge as the proof since the verification of τ will fail if the server has tampered with the database. $\qquad\square$

5.5 INCREMENTAL VDB FRAMEWORK

Chen et al. [52] first introduced a new notion named VDB with incremental updates (Inc-VDB, for short), means that re-computing and updating the ciphertext in VDB are both incremental algorithms, i.e., the client can efficiently perform both operations with previous values, rather than from scratch. The motivation is that the database undergoes frequent while small updates in some scenarios. For example, one anti-virus company outsources its virus database to a cloud server. Also, the company must add the newly discovered viruses to the database everyday. Generally, the daily newly discovered viruses are a very tiny part of whole database and almost all parts of the database remain unchanged. However, the company is still required to *re-compute* and *update* the whole ciphertext everyday (note that the ciphertext is totally different even if the plaintext is modified only 1 bit for almost all provable secure encryption schemes). For a very large database, it is extremely expensive for the resources-constrained client to re-compute and update the ciphertext from scratch each time.

The notion of incremental encryption [15, 16] seems a naive solution for Inc-VDB scheme. For example, if a single block of the data is modified (we can view the data as a sequence of blocks), the client only needs to re-compute the ciphertext on this certain block and the ciphertext of other blocks remains identical [19, 101]. Nevertheless, this incremental encryption method does not provide a full solution for constructing efficient Inc-VDB schemes. The reasons are two-fold: Firstly, previous incremental encryption schemes cannot solve the case of distributed updates on the data. That is, multiple blocks of the plaintext are modified while the modification on each single block is very small. The worst case is that every block of the plaintext is updated while only one bit for each single block is changed. If this case happens, the client must re-compute the whole ciphertext from scratch. Secondly, previous incremental encryption schemes cannot necessarily lead to incremental updates on VDB. That is, the update algorithm of VDB is not incremental and the client still needs to re-compute a new updated token from scratch each time.

Chen et al. [52] proposed a new incremental encryption based on the bit flipping operation and then presented an efficient Inc-VDB framework from vector commitment and the incremental encrypt-then-MAC mode of encryption.

5.5.1 INCREMENTAL ENCRYPTION BASED ON BIT FLIPPING

The proposed incremental encryption based on bit flipping is a main building block to construct Inc-VDB schemes. Actually, it is a general mechanism for converting any provable secure encryption scheme into an incremental one. The construction $\Pi = (\text{KG}, \text{ENC}, \text{DEC}, \text{Inc-ENC}, \text{Inc-DEC})$ is given as follows:

- KG: On input the security parameter k, the key generation algorithm outputs the secret/public key pair (SK, PK). Without loss of generality, let $\Pi_0 = (\text{KG}, \text{ENC}, \text{DEC})$ be any IND-CCA secure (symmetric or asymmetric) encryption scheme and the key is implicit in the notation for simplicity. Trivially, the public key PK is an empty string if Π_0 is a symmetric scheme.

- ENC: On input a message m, the encryption algorithm outputs a ciphertext $c = \text{ENC}(m)$.

- DEC: On input the ciphertext c, the decryption algorithm outputs the message $m = \text{DEC}(c)$.

- Inc-ENC: On input a slightly modified message m', the original message m, and the ciphertext c on m, the incremental encryption algorithm outputs the (incremental) ciphertext $c' = \text{Inc-ENC}(m', c, m) = (c, P)$, where $P = (p_1, p_2, \cdots, p_\omega)$ denotes the bit positions where m' and m have different values, i.e., $m'[p_i] \neq m[p_i]$ for $1 \leq i \leq \omega$.

- Inc-DEC: On input the ciphertext $c' = (c, P)$, the incremental decryption algorithm outputs the message m'. Trivially, it firstly decrypts c to obtain m and then performs the bit flipping operation on the location p_i $(1 \leq i \leq \omega)$ of m.

In the following, we present the formal security proof of our construction.

Theorem 5.11 *If Π_0 is an IND-CCA secure (symmetric or asymmetric) encryption scheme, then Π is also an IND-CCA secure encryption scheme.*

Proof. We prove by contradiction. Assume that there exists a polynomial time IND-CCA adversary $\mathcal{A}$ can successfully attack the scheme Π with a non-negligible probability ϵ in time T, then we can construct another polynomial time IND-CCA adversary $\mathcal{A}_0$ that uses $\mathcal{A}$ as a subroutine to attack the scheme Π_0. Without loss of generality, we assume that $\mathcal{A}$ can make at most $q_1 + q_2$ decryption queries.

Let $c_i' = (c_i, P_i)$ be a decryption query issued by $\mathcal{A}$. Trivially, $\mathcal{A}_0$ can relay the partial decryption query c_i to the challenger $\mathcal{C}$ in Π_0. Suppose the response of $\mathcal{C}$ is m_i, $\mathcal{A}_0$ performs the bit flipping operation on the location P_i of m_i to obtain m_i'. Then $\mathcal{A}_0$ responds m_i' to the query c_i' of $\mathcal{A}$.

After issuing q_1 decryption queries, $\mathcal{A}$ chooses two distinct (challenge) messages $(\mathbf{m}_0', \mathbf{m}_1')$ and sends them to $\mathcal{A}_0$. Similarly, $\mathcal{A}_0$ can compute two corresponding (challenge) messages $(\mathbf{m}_0, \mathbf{m}_1)$ for scheme Π_0, where $\mathbf{m}_b$ ($b \in \{0, 1\}$) is obtained by performing the bit flipping operation on the location $\mathbf{P}$ of $\mathbf{m}_b'$ and $\mathbf{P}$ is some bit positions randomly chosen by $\mathcal{A}_0$.

Let the challenge ciphertext by $\mathcal{C}$ be $\mathbf{c} = \mathsf{ENC}(\mathbf{m}_b)$. Trivially, $\mathcal{A}_0$ can compute the corresponding challenge ciphertext $\mathbf{c}' = (\mathbf{c}, \mathbf{P})$ for $\mathcal{A}$. Then $\mathcal{A}$ can issue further q_2 decryption queries except $\mathbf{c}'$ and $\mathcal{A}_0$ responds in the same way as above.

Finally, $\mathcal{A}$ outputs its guess $b' \in \{0, 1\}$. Then $\mathcal{A}_0$ can replay b' as its guess in the scheme Π_0. Trivially, the success probability of $\mathcal{A}_0$ is also ϵ. $\qquad\square$

As pointed out in [16], incremental encryption leaks some information that is kept secret when using a traditional encryption scheme. In the proposed incremental encryption scheme Inc-ENC, an adversary can determine where a modification takes place, but still cannot determine the symbol being modified (i.e., hide details about the data record m and m'). This is similar to previous incremental encryptions [16, 19, 101]. In order to achieve stronger privacy, it should also encrypt the modified location information P. That is, $\mathsf{Inc\text{-}ENC}(m') = (\mathsf{ENC}(m), \mathsf{ENC}(P))$. On the other hand, though we only focus on the bit flipping operation in our construction, it can be extended to other operations such as insertion, deletion, etc.

On the other hand, we present a method to represent the ciphertext efficiently. Suppose the ciphertext is $(\mathsf{ENC}(m), P_1, \cdots, P_l)$ after performing l rounds of update. We give the following recursive definition if we view P_j as a set:

$$\bar{P}_1 = P_1,$$

$$\bar{P}_{j+1} = \bar{P}_j \oplus P_{j+1} = (\bar{P}_j - P_{j+1}) \cup (P_{j+1} - \bar{P}_j).$$

As a result, the ciphertext is now $(\mathsf{ENC}(m), \bar{P}_l)$ (or $(\mathsf{ENC}(m), \mathsf{ENC}(\bar{P}_l))$ to enhance the privacy). This ensures deletion of the identical positions information of P_j (thus no bit flipping operation is required in these positions) and the ciphertext is also shortened.

5.5.2   INC-VDB FRAMEWORK

Chen et al. [52] introduced the Inc-VDB framework by incorporating the primitive of vector commitment and the encrypt-then-incremental MAC mode of encryption. The main trick is two-fold:

Firstly, the framework uses the above incremental encryption to generate the updated ciphertext v'_x. More precisely, define $v'_x = (v_x, P_x)$, where $P_x = (p_1, p_2, \cdots, p_\omega)$ denotes the bit positions where m'_x and m_x have different values, i.e, $m'_x[p_i] \neq m_x[p_i]$ for $1 \leq i \leq \omega$. Trivially, given $v'_x = (v_x, P_x)$, the client firstly decrypts v_x to obtain m_x, and then performs the bit flipping operation on the positions of P_x to obtain m'_x. Since the bit flipping operation is extremely fast, the computation overhead of decrypting v'_x is almost the same as that of decrypting v_x. Moreover, it requires much less storage since $|P_x| << |v'_x|$ (note that we only consider the case of incremental updates).

Secondly, the framework utilizes the encrypt-then-incremental MAC mode of encryption [19], i.e., an incremental encryption together with an incremental MAC of the ciphertext (the encrypt-then-MAC approach [29]), to generate the updated token t'_x. Also, it uses an incremental version of the BLS signature scheme [27] to substitute the incremental MAC. For every update, the client first verifies the current BLS signature on the commitment C_R and all the current modifications $(P_x^{(1)}, \cdots, P_x^{(T)})$ of the data record v_x, where $P_x^{(i)}$ denotes the modification in the i-th update for $1 \leq i \leq T$. This ensures that the current database is not tampered with by the server.[9] If the verification holds, the client then sends a new modification $P_x^{(T+1)}$ and the corresponding (incremental) BLS signature to the server.

Since the framework also uses the signature to achieve the integrity of the database, it is essential to invoke the previous signatures given to the server. The trick is that the server computes a BLS signature σ on all counters T_x for $1 \leq x \leq q$, where T_x denotes the update number of each index x. After an update on the record v_x is accomplished, let $T_x \leftarrow T_x + 1$. Then the server computes an incremental BLS signature on the updated counters (note that only the value of T_x is slightly modified). Given a previous signature σ on the count T_x, the client can reject it by providing a new signature σ' on the latest counter T'_x since $T_x < T'_x$. Note that the server cannot deny his signature, therefore this is a proof that the server is dishonest when a dispute occurred.

Note that the paradigm by incorporating the primitive of vector commitment and the encrypt-then-incremental MAC mode of encryption actually provides a general framework for constructing Inc-VDB schemes. That is, if we use different vector commitment schemes and incremental encryption/signature schemes, we can obtain various constructions for Inc-VDB schemes.

---

[9]Bellare, Goldreich, and Goldwasser pointed out that some incremental signature schemes may suffer from the so-called substitution attack in some scenarios. However, it assumed that the adversary can successfully tamper with the data and the signer does not check the corresponding signatures. Obviously, the attack does not work in our scheme.

5.5.3 A CONCRETE INC-VDB SCHEME

In this section, we introduce a concrete Inc-VDB scheme based on the CDH assumption [52].

- **Setup**(1^k, DB): Let k be a security parameter. Let the database be DB $= (x, v_x)$ for $1 \leq x \leq q$. Let $\mathbb{G}_1$ and $\mathbb{G}_2$ be two cyclic multiplicative groups of prime order p equipped with a bilinear pairing $e : \mathbb{G}_1 \times \mathbb{G}_1 \to \mathbb{G}_2$. Let g be a generator of $\mathbb{G}_1$. Let $\mathcal{H} : \mathbb{G}_1 \times \{0,1\}^* \to \mathbb{G}_1$ be a cryptographic hash function. Randomly choose q elements $z_i \in_R \mathbb{Z}_p$ and compute $h_i = g^{z_i}$, $h_{i,j} = g^{z_i z_j}$, where $1 \leq i, j \leq q$ and $i \neq j$. Set PP $= (p, q, \mathbb{G}_1, \mathbb{G}_2, \mathcal{H}, e, g, \{h_i\}_{1 \leq i \leq q}, \{h_{i,j}\}_{1 \leq i,j \leq q, i \neq j})$, and the message space $\mathcal{M} = \mathbb{Z}_p$.[10]

  Let $(\alpha, \mathsf{Y} = g^\alpha)$ and $(\beta, \mathsf{Z} = g^\beta)$ be the secret/public key pair of the client C and server S, respectively, where $\alpha, \beta \in_R \mathbb{Z}_p^*$. Trivially, the validity of Y and Z are ensured by the corresponding certificate of a trusted third party, i.e, certificate authority. Let $\mathsf{C}_R = \prod_{i=1}^q h_i^{v_i}$ be the root commitment on the database record vector $(v_1, v_2, \cdots, v_q)$. For $1 \leq x \leq q$, let T_x be a counter for index x with the initial value 0 and $H_x^{(0)} = \mathcal{H}(\mathsf{C}_R, x, 0)^\alpha$. S can use the batch verification technique of BLS signatures [43] to ensure the validity of $H_x^{(0)}$ for $1 \leq x \leq q$, which requires only the workload of two pairings. Then S computes a signature $\sigma = \mathcal{H}(\mathsf{C}_R, 0, 0, \cdots, 0)^\beta$ on C_R and all initial counters $(0, 0, \cdots, 0)$ (note that all T_x has an initial value 0). Also, set aux $= \{\mathsf{aux}_1, \cdots, \mathsf{aux}_q\}$, where $\mathsf{aux}_x = (H_x^{(0)}, 0)$ for $1 \leq x \leq q$.

  Define PK $= (\mathsf{PP}, \mathsf{C}_R, \mathsf{aux}, \mathsf{DB})$ and SK $= \alpha$.

- Query(PK, x): Assume that the current public key PK $= (\mathsf{PP}, \mathsf{C}_R, \mathsf{aux}, \mathsf{DB})$. Given a query index x, S computes $\pi_x = \prod_{1 \leq j \leq q, j \neq x} h_{x,j}^{v_j}$ and returns the proofs

$$\tau = (v_x, \pi_x, H_x^{(T_x)}, P_x^{(1)}, \cdots, P_x^{(T_x)}, T_x).$$

  Note that the proof $\pi_x = \prod_{1 \leq j \leq q, j \neq x} h_{x,j}^{v_j}$ is always identical for all queries to the same index x. Therefore, S only needs to compute π_x once for the first query on index x (this is different from the scheme [41]). Trivially, S requires much less computational overhead for the query algorithms.

- Verify(PK, x, τ): Parse the proofs $\tau = (v_x, \pi_x, H_x^{(T_x)}, P_x^{(1)}, \cdots, P_x^{(T_x)}, T_x)$. If the counter T_x in τ is less than the one in σ that C stored locally, C rejects the proofs τ. Otherwise, C can verify the validity of τ by checking whether the following two equations $e(\mathsf{C}_R / h_x^{v_x}, h_x) = e(\pi_x, g)$ and $e(H_x^{(T_x)}, g) = e(\mathcal{H}(\mathsf{C}_R, x, P_x^{(1)}, \cdots, P_x^{(T_x)}, T_x), \mathsf{Y})$ hold. If the proofs τ are valid, C accepts them and outputs $v_x^{(T_x)} = (v_x, P_x^{(1)}, \cdots, P_x^{(T_x)})$. Otherwise, outputs an error $\perp$.

- Inc-Update(SK, x, $P_x^{(T_x+1)}$): To update the record of index x, C firstly retrieves the current record $v_x^{(T_x)}$ from S. That is, C obtains $\tau \leftarrow$ Query(PK, x) from S and checks that

---

[10]Though the message space $\mathcal{M}$ in this construction is $\mathbb{Z}_p$, it can be easily extended to support possibly large payload v_i by using a collision-resistant hash function $H : \{0,1\}^* \to \mathbb{Z}_p$.

Verify(PK, x, τ) = $v_x^{(T_x)} \neq \perp$. Then C computes the incremental signature

$$t_x' = H_x^{(T_x+1)} = \mathcal{H}(\mathsf{C}_R, x, P_x^{(1)}, \cdots, P_x^{(T_x+1)}, T_x + 1)^\alpha$$

and then sends $(t_x', P_x^{(T_x+1)})$ to S. If t_x' is valid, then S adds $P_x^{(T_x+1)}$ to the record of index x, and updates aux_x in PK, i.e., $\mathrm{aux}_x \leftarrow (t_x', P_x^{(1)}, \cdots, P_x^{(T_x+1)}, T_x + 1)$. Also, S computes an updated incremental signature $\sigma = \mathcal{H}(\mathsf{C}_R, T_1, T_2, \cdots, T_x + 1, \cdots, T_q)^\beta$ and sends it to C. If σ is valid, C updates it together with $T_x + 1$ locally. Finally, set $T_x \leftarrow T_x + 1$.

Remark 7. The storage overhead of the client in our construction is all counters T_x and the latest BLS signature σ. Note that the number of T_x is dependent on q, we estimate the storage overload of client for very large q.

Assume that $q = 10^8$ and the counter T_x for each index x is 10^6 (that is, the database has 10^8 records and for each index x it has been updated 1 million times). This means that the total number of update for the database is 10^{6*10^8} (this is a giant updates number in real applications). However, the storage of the client is only about $7 * 10^8$ bits (less that 700 M). It is still tolerable even for a resource-limited client.

In the following, a new solution is given in order to further reduce the storage overload of the client. The trick is to still use vector commitment. The server computes the signature $\sigma = \mathcal{H}(\mathsf{C}_R, \mathsf{C}_T)^\beta$, where C_T is the vector commitment on all counters $(T_1, T_2, \cdots, T_q)$. Therefore, the client only requires storing σ and C_T, and the storage overhead is independent of q. Trivially, the server should provide a valid opening of C_T as a proof during the verification phase. Due to the property of vector commitment, the update of C_T is still incremental.

CHAPTER 6

Conclusion and Future Works

Outsourcing computation is a fruitful and long-standing research topic in the academic community. With the development of cloud computing and big data, we believe that more and more researchers will focus on this hot topic. In this book, we present research progress on outsourcing computation, while it is far from complete due to space and time constraints.

In the following, we present some (possible) future works and open problems in outsourcing computation.

- In the outsourcing scientific computations, how do we achieve the CCA security for the inputs? A totally random blinding or disguise technique seems not to work. For example, if we blind a dense matrix with rank n by multiplying a randomly chosen dense matrix, the computation overload should be n^3. In this sense, we should find some more efficient algorithms which can still achieve the strongest security notions.

- Is it possible to find an efficient algorithm for securely outsourcing the cryptographic operations by only using an untrusted server? Note that the algorithm should also only require one round of interaction between the server and the client. We left it as an open problem.

- The system parameters in current VDB schemes are proportional to the number of database indices. Thus, the constructions are given in the amortized model. It is interesting to propose a construction (or a framework) for efficient VDB with constant system parameters. Besides, the current VDB schemes do not support the insertion kind of update since the number of database indices is fixed in advance. Therefore, an interesting open problem is to propose an efficient VDB scheme supporting all kinds of update operations (insertion, deletion, and replacement).

- How do we detect the misbehavior of an untrusted server in the multiple results of outsourcing computations? For example, the computation task is to find all collisions of one-way function or to find all solutions of a large-scale linear equation (the solution is not unique). In these scenarios, the servers may not send all the computation results to the client. In the worst case, the untrusted server just responds with an empty set. The idea of ringer is a partial solution that is only suitable for an "inversion of one-way function" class of outsourcing computations. Is there any other efficient solution to solve this problem by using some new primitives, such as verifiably searchable encryption?

- It seems that VDB is closely related to proof of retrievability (PoR) [55, 64, 86, 119, 129]. What is the essential relationship between the two primitives? On the other hand, the current VDB schemes rarely consider the privacy of the clients, especially in the multi-client scenarios. Therefore, it is interesting to design efficient privacy-preserving VDB schemes using some new cryptographic primitives.

- Backes, Fiore, and Reischuk [13] firstly introduced the idea of outsourcing big data. That is, the size of outsourced data is very huge while not fixed beforehand (the data may be changing and increasing). Currently, we are facing the era of big data. Thus, it is interesting to construct more flexible and efficient outsourcing schemes for big data.

Bibliography

[1] M.J. Atallah and K.B. Frikken. Securely outsourcing linear algebra computations. *Proceedings of the 5th ACM Symposium on Information, Computer and Communications Security (ASIACCS)*, pp. 48–59, 2010. DOI: 10.1145/1755688.1755695. 3, 19

[2] M. Abadi, J. Feigenbaum, and J. Kilian. On hiding information from an oracle. *Proceedings of the 19th Annual ACM Symposium on Theory of Computing (STOC)*, pp. 195–203, 1987. DOI: 10.1145/28395.28417. 19

[3] M.J. Atallah and J. Li. Secure outsourcing of sequence comparisons. *International Journal of Information Security*, 4(4), pp. 277–287, 2005. DOI: 10.1007/s10207-005-0070-3. 19

[4] B. Andrei and M. Michael. Network applications of bloom filters: A survey. *Internet Mathematics*, 1(4), pp. 485–509, 2004. DOI: 10.1080/15427951.2004.10129096. 17

[5] G. Ateniese and B. de Medeiros. Identity-based chameleon hash and applications. *Financial Cryptography (FC)*, LNCS 3110, Springer, pp. 164–180, 2004. DOI: 10.1007/978-3-540-27809-2_19. 38

[6] G. Ateniese and B. de Medeiros. On the key-exposure problem in chameleon hashes. *Security in Communication Networks (SCN)*, LNCS 3352, Springer, pp. 165–179, 2005. DOI: 10.1007/978-3-540-30598-9_12. 38

[7] M.J. Atallah, K.N. Pantazopoulos, J.R. Rice, and E.H. Spafford. Secure outsourcing of scientific computations. *Advances in Computers*, vol. 54, pp. 216–272, 2001. DOI: 10.1016/s0065-2458(01)80019-x. 3, 19, 20, 22, 23

[8] D. Benjamin and M.J. Atallah. Private and cheating-free outsourcing of algebraic computations. *Proceedings of the 6th Annual Conference on Privacy, Security and Trust (PST)*, pp. 240–245, 2008. DOI: 10.1109/pst.2008.12. 19

[9] G. Brassard, D. Chaum, and C. Crepeau. Minimum disclosure proofs of knowledge. *Journal of Computer and System Sciences*, 37(2), pp. 156–189, 1988. DOI: 10.1016/0022-0000(88)90005-0. 38

[10] F. Bao, R. Deng, and H. Zhu. Variations of Diffie-Hellman Problem. *Information and Communications Security (ICS)*, LNCS 2836, pp. 301–312, Springer, 2003. DOI: 10.1007/978-3-540-39927-8_28. 11

[11] D. Boneh and M. Franklin. Identity-based encryption from the Weil pairings. *Advances in Cryptology-Crypto 2001*, LNCS 2139, pp. 213–229, Springer, 2001. DOI: 10.1007/3-540-44647-8_13. 12

[12] D. Beaver, J. Feigenbaum, J. Kilian, and P. Rogaway. Locally random reductions: Improvements and applications. *Journal of Cryptology*, 10(1), pp. 17–36, 1997. DOI: 10.1007/s001459900017. 34

[13] M. Backes, D. Fiore, and R.M. Reischuk. Verifiable Delegation of Computation on Outsourced Data. *Proceedings of the ACM Conference on Computer and Communications Security (CCS)*, pp. 863–874, ACM, 2013. DOI: 10.1145/2508859.2516681. 3, 66

[14] M. Ben-Or, S. Goldwasser, J. Kilian, and A. Wigderson. Multi-prover interactive proofs: How to remove intractability assumptions. *Proceedings of the ACM Symposium on Theory of Computing (STOC)*, pp. 113–131, 1988. DOI: 10.1145/62212.62223. 33

[15] M. Bellare, O. Goldreich, and S. Goldwasser. Incremental cryptography: The case of hashing and signing. *Advances in Cryptology-CRYPTO 1994*, LNCS 2836, pp. 216–233, Springer, 1994. DOI: 10.1007/3-540-48658-5_22. 58

[16] M. Bellare, O. Goldreich, and S. Goldwasser. Incremental Cryptography and Application to Virus Protection. *Proceedings of the 27th ACM Symposium on the Theory of Computing (STOC)*, pp. 45–56, 1995. DOI: 10.1145/225058.225080. 58, 60

[17] D. Boneh, E.J. Goh, and K. Nissim. Evaluating 2-dnf formulas on ciphertexts. *Theory of Cryptography*, pp. 325–341, Springer, 2005. DOI: 10.1007/978-3-540-30576-7_18. 12

[18] S. Benabbas, R. Gennaro, and Y. Vahlis. Verifiable delegation of computation over large datasets. *Advances in Cryptology-CRYPTO 2011*, LNCS 6841, pp. 111–131, Springer, 2011. DOI: 10.1007/978-3-642-22792-9_7. 12, 15, 45, 46, 47, 52, 53, 54

[19] E. Buonanno, J. Katz, and M. Yung. Incremental Unforgeable Encryption. *Fast Software Encryption (FSE)*, LNCS 2355, pp. 109–124, Springer, 2002. DOI: 10.1007/3-540-45473-x_9. 59, 60, 61

[20] M. Benzi. Preconditioning Techniques for Large Linear Systems: A Survey. *Journal of Computational Physics*, 182, pp. 418–477, 2002. DOI: 10.1006/jcph.2002.7176. 23, 26

[21] D. Boneh. Twenty years of attacks on the RSA cryptosystem. *Notices of the American Mathematical Society*, 46(2), pp. 203–213, 1999. 29

[22] M. Blanton. Improved conditional e-payments. *Applied Cryptography and Network Security (ACNS)*, LNCS 5037, pp. 188–206, Springer, 2008. DOI: 10.1007/978-3-540-68914-0_12. 4

[23] M. Blanton, M.J. Atallah, K.B. Frikken, and Q. Malluhi. Secure and efficient outsourcing of sequence comparisons. *ESORICS 2012*, LNCS 7459, pp. 505–522, Springer, 2012. DOI: 10.1007/978-3-642-33167-1_29. 19

[24] B.H. Bloom. Space/Time trade-offs in hash coding with allowable Errors, *Communications of the ACM*, 13(7), pp. 422–426, 1970. DOI: 10.1145/362686.362692. 17

[25] M. Blum, M. Luby, and R. Rubinfeld. Program result checking against adaptive programs and in cryptographic settings. *DIMACS Series in Discrete Mathematics and Theoretical Computer Science*, pp. 107–118, 1991. 33

[26] M. Blum, M. Luby, and R. Rubinfeld. Self-testing/correcting with applications to numerical problems. *Journal of Computer and System Science*, 47(3), pp. 549–595, 1993. DOI: 10.1016/0022-0000(93)90044-w. 33

[27] D. Boneh, B. Lynn, and H. Shacham. Short signatures from the Weil pairings. *Advances in Cryptology-Asiacrypt*, LNCS 2248, pp. 514–532, Springer, 2001. DOI: 10.1007/3-540-45682-1_30. 12, 61

[28] F. Bonomi, M. Mitzenmacher, R. Panigrahy, S. Singh, and G. Varghese. An Improved Construction for Counting Bloom Filters. *Algorithms CESA*, pp. 684–695, Springer, 2006. DOI: 10.1007/11841036_61. 17

[29] M. Bellare and C. Namprempre. Authenticated Encryption: Relations Among Notions and Analysis of the Generic Composition Paradigm. *Advances in Cryptology-Asiacrypt*, LNCS 1976, pp. 531–545, Springer, 2000. DOI: 10.1007/3-540-44448-3_41. 61

[30] P. Barreto and M. Naehrig. Pairing-friendly elliptic curves of prime order. *Selected Areas in Cryptography*, pp. 319–331, Springer, 2006. DOI: 10.1007/11693383_22. 43

[31] V. Boyko, M. Peinado, and R. Venkatesan. Speeding up discrete log and factoring based schemes via precomputations. *Advances in Cryptology-Eurocrypt*, LNCS 1403, pp. 221–232, Springer, 1998. DOI: 10.1007/bfb0054129. 30, 34

[32] D. Boneh and B. Waters. Conjunctive, subset, and range queries on encrypted data. *Theory of Cryptography*, LNCS 4392, pp. 535–554, Springer, 2007. DOI: 10.1007/978-3-540-70936-7_29. 12

[33] D. Chaum. Blind signature for untraceable payments. *Advances in Cryptology-Eurocrypt*, pp. 199–203, 1982. DOI: 10.1007/978-1-4757-0602-4_18. 20

[34] D. Chaum and T. Pedersen. Wallet databases with observers. *Advances in Cryptology-Crypto*, LNCS 740, pp. 89–105, Springer, 1993. DOI: 10.1007/3-540-48071-4_7. 30

[35] S. Chow, M. Au, and W. Susilo. Server-aided signatures verification secure against collusion attack. *Proceedings of the 6th ACM Symposium on Information, Computer and Communications Security (ASIACCS)*, pp. 401–405, 2011. DOI: 10.1145/1966913.1966967.

[36] J. Cha and J.H. Cheon. An identity-based signature from gap Diffie CHellman groups. *PKC 2003*, LNCS 2567, pp. 18–30, Springer, 2003. DOI: 10.1007/3-540-36288-6_2. 12

[37] B. Chevallier-Mames, J. Coron, N. McCullagh, D. Naccache, and M. Scott. Secure delegation of elliptic-curve pairing. *Smart Card Research and Advanced Application*, LNCS 6035, pp. 24–35, Springer, 2010. DOI: 10.1007/978-3-642-12510-2_3. 30, 40

[38] R. Cramer and I. Damgard. Multiparty computation, an introduction. *Contemporary Cryptology*, pp. 41–87, 2005. DOI: 10.1007/3-7643-7394-6_2. 2

[39] S. Canard, J. Devigne, and O. Sanders. Delegating a pairing can be both secure and efficient. *Applied Cryptography and Network Security*, pp. 549–565, Springer, 2014. DOI: 10.1007/978-3-319-07536-5_32. 43

[40] D. Catalano, D. Fiore, and M. Messina. Zero-knowledge sets with short proofs. *Advances in Cryptology-EUROCRYPT*, LNCS 4965, pp. 433–450, Springer, 2008. DOI: 10.1007/978-3-540-78967-3_25. 14

[41] D. Catalano and D. Fiore. Vector commitments and their applications. *PKC 2013*, LNCS 7778, pp. 55–72, Springer, 2013. DOI: 10.1007/978-3-642-36362-7_5. 14, 15, 45, 46, 51, 57, 62

[42] X. Chen, F. Zhang, and K. Kim. Chameleon Hashing without Key Exposure. *Information Security Conference*, LNCS 3225, pp. 135–148, Springer, 2004. DOI: 10.1007/978-3-540-30144-8_8. 38

[43] J. Camenisch, S. Hohenberger, and M. Pedersen. Batch Verification of Short Signatures. *Advances in Cryptology-EUROCRYPT*, LNCS 4515, pp. 246–263, Springer, 2007. DOI: 10.1007/978-3-540-72540-4_14. 62

[44] X. Chen, F. Zhang, W. Susilo, and Y. Mu. Efficient generic online/off-line signatures without key exposure. *Applied Cryptography and Network Security (ACNS)*, LNCS 4521, pp. 18–30, Springer, 2007. DOI: 10.1007/978-3-540-72738-5_2. 38

[45] X. Chen, J. Li, and W. Susilo. Efficient Fair Conditional Payments for Outsourcing Computations. *IEEE Transactions on Information Forensics and Security*, 7(6), pp. 1687–1694, 2012. DOI: 10.1109/tifs.2012.2210880. 3, 4

[46] X. Chen, F. Zhang, W. Susilo, H. Tian, J. Li, and K. Kim. Identity-based chameleon hashing and signatures without key exposure. *Information Sciences*, 265, pp. 198–210, 2014. DOI: 10.1016/j.ins.2013.12.020. 38

[47] X. Chen, J. Li, X. Huang, J. Ma, and W. Lou. New publicly verifiable databases with efficient updates. *IEEE Transactions on Dependable Secure Computing*, 12(5), pp. 546–556, 2015. DOI: 10.1109/tdsc.2014.2366471. 51, 52, 54, 56

[48] X. Chen, W. Susilo, F. Zhang, H. Tian, and J. Li. Identity-Based Trapdoor Mercurial Commitment and Applications. Theoretical *Computer Science*, 412(39), pp. 5498–5512, 2011. DOI: 10.1016/j.tcs.2011.05.031. 14

[49] X. Chen, J. Li, J. Ma, Q. Tang, and W. Lou. New algorithms for secure outsourcing of modular exponentiations. *ESORICS*, LNCS 7459, pp. 541–556, Springer, 2012. DOI: 10.1007/978-3-642-33167-1_31. 3, 33, 35, 38, 39

[50] X. Chen, J. Li, X. Huang, J. Li, Y. Xiang, and D. Wong. Secure Outsourced Attribute-based Signatures. *IEEE Transactions on Parallel and Distributed Systems*, 25(12), pp. 3285–3294, 2014. DOI: 10.1109/tpds.2013.2295809. 3

[51] X. Chen, X. Huang, J. Li, J. Ma, and W. Lou. New Algorithms for Secure Outsourcing of Large-scale Systems of Linear Equations. *IEEE Transactions on Information and Forensics Security*, 10(1), pp. 69–78, 2015. DOI: 10.1109/tifs.2014.2363765. 20, 24

[52] X. Chen, J. Li, J. Weng, J. Ma, and W. Lou. Verifiable Computation over Large Database with Incremental Updates. *ESORICS*, LNCS 8712, pp. 148–162, Springer, 2014. DOI: 10.1007/978-3-319-11203-9_9. 58, 59, 61, 62

[53] X. Chen, W. Susilo, J. Li, D.S. Wong, J. Ma, S. Tang, and Q. Tang. Efficient algorithms for secure outsourcing of bilinear pairings. *Theoretical Computer Science*, 562, pp. 112–121, 2015. DOI: 10.1016/j.tcs.2014.09.038. 41, 42

[54] X. Chen et al. Publicly Verifiable Databases with All Efficient Operations, manuscipt. DOI: 10.1109/tdsc.2014.2366471. 18

[55] R. Curtmola, O. Khan, and R. Burns. Robust remote data checking. *Proceeding of the 4th ACM Workshop on Storage Security and Survivability (StorageSS)*, pp. 63–68, 2008. DOI: 10.1145/1456469.1456481. 66

[56] J. Camenisch, M. Kohlweiss, and C. Soriente. An accumulator based on bilinear maps and efficient revocation for anonymous credentials. *PKC*, LNCS 5443, pp. 481–500, Springer, 2009. DOI: 10.1007/978-3-642-00468-1_27. 45

[57] J. Camenisch and A. Lysyanskaya. Dynamic accumulators and application to efficient revocation of anonymous credentials. *Advances in Cryptology-CRYPTO*, LNCS 2442, pp. 61–76, Springer, 2002. DOI: 10.1007/3-540-45708-9_5. 45

[58] R. Canetti, B. Riva, and G.N. Rothblum. Practical delegation of computation using multiple servers. *Proceedings of the 18th ACM Conference on Computer and Communications Security (CCS)*, pp. 445–454, 2011. DOI: 10.1145/2046707.2046759. 4, 7

[59] Y. Chen and R. Sion. Costs and Security in Clouds. *Secure Cloud Computing*, pp. 31–56, Springer, 2014. DOI: 10.1007/978-1-4614-9278-8_2. 1

[60] Top Threats Working Group. The notorious nine: cloud computing top threats in 2013. *Cloud Security Alliance Technical Report*, 2013.

[61] B. Carbunar and M. Tripunitara. Conditioal payments for computing markets. *Cryptology and Network Security (CANS)*, LNCS 5339, pp. 317–331, Springer, 2008. DOI: 10.1007/978-3-540-89641-8_23. 4

[62] B. Carbunar and M. Tripunitara. Fair payments for outsourced computations. *Proceedings of the 7th Annual IEEE Communications Society Conference on Sensor, Mesh and Ad Hoc Communications and Networks (SECON)*, pp. 529–537, 2010. DOI: 10.1109/secon.2010.5508202. 4

[63] W. Diffie and M.E. Hellman. New directions in cryptography. *IEEE Transactions in Information Theory*, 22(6), pp. 644–654, 1976. DOI: 10.1109/tit.1976.1055638. 29

[64] Y. Dodis, S. Vadhan, and D. Wichs. Proofs of retrivability via hardness amplification. *TCC*, pp. 109–127, Springer, 2009. DOI: 10.1007/978-3-642-00457-5_8. 66

[65] D. Eppstein and M.T. Goodrich. Straggler Identification in Round-Trip Data Streams via Newton's Identities and Invertible Bloom Filters. *IEEE Transactions on Knowledge and Data Engineering*, 23(2), pp. 297–306, 2011. DOI: 10.1109/tkde.2010.132. 17

[66] S. Even, O. Goldreich, and S. Micali. On-line/Off-line digital signatures. *Journal of Cryptology*, 9(1), pp. 35–67, Springer, 1996. DOI: 10.1007/bf02254791. 29, 34

[67] M. Fischlin and R. Fischlin. Efficient non-malleable commitment schemes. *Advances in Cryptology*, LNCS 1880, pp. 413–431, Springer, 2000. DOI: 10.1007/3-540-44598-6_26. 54

[68] K. Forsman, W. Gropp, L. Kettunen, D. Levine, and J. Salonen. Solution of dense systems of linear equations arising from integral-equation formulations. *IEEE Antennas and Propagation Magazine*, 37(6), pp. 96–100, 1995. DOI: 10.1109/74.482076. 23

[69] C. Gentry. A fully homomorphic encryption scheme. Ph.D. thesis, Stanford University, 2009. 8

[70] C. Gentry. Fully homomorphic encryption using ideal lattices. *Proceedings of the ACM Symposium on the Theory of Computing (STOC)*, pp. 169–178, 2009. DOI: 10.1145/1536414.1536440. 8

[71] M. Girault and D. Lefranc. Server-aided verification: theory and practice. *Advances in Cryptology-Asiacrypt*, LNCS 3788, pp. 605–623, Springer, 2005. DOI: 10.1007/11593447_33. 30, 34

[72] S. Galbraith, K. Paterson, and N. Smart. Pairings for cryptographers. *Discrete Applied Mathematics*, 156(16), pp. 3113–3121, 2008. DOI: 10.1016/j.dam.2007.12.010. 40

[73] S. Goldwasser, Y.T. Kalai, and G.N. Rothblum. Delegating computation: interactive proofs for muggles. *Proceedings of the ACM Symposium on the Theory of Computing (STOC)*, pp. 113–122, 2008. DOI: 10.1145/1374376.1374396. 4

[74] R. Gennaro, C. Gentry, and B. Parno. Non-interactive verifiable computing: Outsourcing computation to untrusted workers. *Advances in Cryptology-CRYPTO*, pp. 465–482, Springer, 2010. DOI: 10.1007/978-3-642-14623-7_25. 1, 4, 5, 7, 8, 48

[75] J. Groth, R. Ostrovsky, and A. Sahai. Perfect non-interactive zero knowledge for NP. *Advances in Cryptology-EUROCRYPT*, LNCS 4004, pp. 339–358, Springer, 2006. DOI: 10.1007/11761679_21. 12

[76] J. Groth and A. Sahai. Efficient non-interactive proof systems for bilinear groups. *Advances in Cryptology-EUROCRYPT*, LNCS 4965, pp. 415–432, Springer, 2008. DOI: 10.1007/978-3-540-78967-3_24. 12

[77] S. Goldwasser, S. Micali, and C. Rackoff. The knowledge complexity of interactive proof-systems. *SIAM Journal on Computing*, 18(1), pp. 186–208, 1989. DOI: 10.1137/0218012.

[78] O. Goldreich, S. Micali, and A. Wigderson. How to play any mental game. *Proceedings of the 19th Annual ACM Symposium on Theory of Computing*, pp. 218–229, 1987. DOI: 10.1145/28395.28420. 6

[79] P. Golle and I. Mironov. Uncheatable distributed computations. *CT-RSA*, LNCS 2020, pp. 425–440, Springer, 2001. DOI: 10.1007/3-540-45353-9_31. 4, 7

[80] J. Garay, P. MacKenzie, and K. Yang. Strengthening zero-knowledge protocols using signatures. *Advances in Cryptology-Eurocrypt*, LNCS 2656, pp. 177–194, Springer, 2003. DOI: 10.1007/3-540-39200-9_11. 38

[81] S. Galbraith, K. Paterson, and N. Smart. Pairings for cryptographers. *Discrete Applied Mathematics*, 156(16), pp. 3113–3121, 2008. DOI: 10.1016/j.dam.2007.12.010. 12

[82] S. Hohenberger and A. Lysyanskaya. How to securely outsource cryptographic computations. *Theory of Cryptography*, LNCS 3378, pp. 264–282, Springer, 2005. DOI: 10.1007/978-3-540-30576-7_15. 4, 5, 7, 30, 33, 34, 35, 36, 38, 40

[83] R.A. Horn and C.R. Johnson. *Matrix Analysis*. Cambridge University Press, 1985. 25

[84] H. Hacigumus, B. Iyer, and S. Mehrotra. Providing database as a service. *Proceedings of the 18th International Conference on Data Engineering*, pp. 29–38, IEEE, 2002. DOI: 10.1109/icde.2002.994695. 45

[85] J.J. Rotman. *A First Course in Abstract Algebra*, 3rd ed., Prentice Hall, Upper Saddle River, New Jersey, pp. 127, 2005. 13

[86] A. Juels and B.S. Kaliski. PORs: proofs of retrievalibity for large files. *Proceedings of the 14th ACM Conference on Computer and Communications Security (CCS)*, pp. 584–597, 2007. DOI: 10.1145/1315245.1315317. 66

[87] J. Kilian. A note on efficient zero-knowledge proofs and arguments. *Proceedings of the ACM Symposium on Theory of Computing (STOC)*, pp. 723–732, 1992. DOI: 10.1145/129712.129782. 4

[88] J. Kilian. Improved efficient arguments (preliminary version). *Advances in Cryptology-Crypto*, pp. 311–324, Springer, 1995. 4

[89] T. Kleinjung, K. Aoki, J. Franke, et al. Factorization of a 768-bit RSA modulus. *Advances in Cryptology-Crypto*, LNCS 6223, pp. 333–350, Springer, 2010. DOI: 10.1007/978-3-642-14623-7_18. 1

[90] H. Krawczyk and T. Rabin. Chameleon hashing and signatures. *NDSS*, pp. 143–154, 2000. 38

[91] J. Katz, A. Sahai, and B. Waters. Predicate encryption supporting disjunctions, polynomial equations, and inner products. *Advances in Cryptology-EUROCRYPT*, LNCS 4965, pp. 146–162, 2008. DOI: 10.1007/978-3-540-78967-3_9. 12

[92] J. Li, X. Huang, J. Li, X. Chen, and Y. Xiang. Securely Outsourcing Attribute-Based Encryption with Checkability. *IEEE Transactions on Parallel and Distributed Systems*, 25(8), pp. 2201–2210, 2014. DOI: 10.1109/tpds.2013.271. 3

[93] A. Lathey, P. Atrey, and N. Joshi. Homomorphic low pass filtering on encrypted multimedia over cloud. *IEEE International Conference on Semantic Computing*, pp. 310–313, 2013. DOI: 10.1109/icsc.2013.60. 19

[94] A.K. Lenstra and E.R. Verheul. Selecting cryptographic key sizes. *Journal of Cryptology*, 14(4), pp. 255–293, Springer, 2001. DOI: 10.1007/s00145-001-0009-4. 29

[95] B. Libert and M. Yung. Concise mercurial vector commitments and independent zero-knowledge sets with short proofs. *Theory of Cryptography*, LNCS 5978, pp. 499–517, Springer, 2010. DOI: 10.1007/978-3-642-11799-2_30. 14

[96] S. Micali. CS proofs. *Proceedings of the 35th Annual Symposium on Foundations of Computer Science (FOCS)*, pp. 436–453, 1994. 4

[97] T. Matsumoto, K. Kato, and H. Imai. Speeding up secret computations with insecure auxiliary devices. *Advances in Cryptology-Crypto*, LNCS 403, pp. 497–506, 1988. DOI: 10.1007/0-387-34799-2_35. 30, 34

[98] C.U. Martel, G. Nuckolls, P.T. Devanbu, M. Gertz, A. Kwong, and S.G. Stubblebine. A general model for authenticated data structures. *Algorithmica*, 39(1), pp. 21–41, Springer, 2004. DOI: 10.1007/s00453-003-1076-8. 45

[99] A. Menezes, P. van Oorschot, and S. Vanstone. *Handbook of Applied Cryptography*. CRC Press, 1996. DOI: 10.1201/9781439821916. 39

[100] M. Mohanty, W. Ooi, and P. Atrey. Scale me, crop me, know me not: Supporting scaling and cropping in secret image sharing. *IEEE International Conference on Multimedia and Expo*, pp. 1–6, 2013. DOI: 10.1109/icme.2013.6607567. 19

[101] I. Mironov, O. Pandey, O. Reingold, and G. Segev. Incremental Deterministic Public-Key Encryption. *Advances in Cryptology-Eurocrypt*, LNCS 7237, pp. 628–644, Springer, 2012. DOI: 10.1007/978-3-642-29011-4_37. 59, 60

[102] E. Mykletun, M. Narasimha, and G. Tsudik. Signature bouquets: Immutability for aggregated/condensed signatures. *Proceedings of the 9th European Symposium on Research in Computer Security (ESORICS)*, pp. 160–176, Springer, 2004. DOI: 10.1007/978-3-540-30108-0_10. 45

[103] S. Micali, M. Rabin, and J. Kilian. Zero-knowledge sets. *Proceedings of the 44th Annual IEEE Symposium on Foundations of Computer Science (FOCS)*, pp. 80–91, IEEE, 2003. DOI: 10.1109/sfcs.2003.1238183. 14

[104] E. Mykletun and G. Tsudik. Aggregation queries in the database-as-a-service model. *Proceedings of the 20th IFIP WG 11.3 Working Conference on Data and Applications Security*, pp. 89–103, Springer, 2006. DOI: 10.1007/11805588_7. 45

[105] L. Nguyen. Accumulators from bilinear pairings and applications. *CT-RSA*, LNCS 3376, pp. 75–292, Springer, 2005. DOI: 10.1007/978-3-540-30574-3_19. 45

[106] P.Q. Nguyen, I.E. Shparlinski, and J. Stern. Distribution of modular sums and the security of server aided exponentiation. *Proceedings of the Workshop on Cryptography and Computational Number Theory*, pp. 1–16, 1999. DOI: 10.1007/978-3-0348-8295-8_24. 34

[107] M. Naor and K. Nissim. Certificate revocation and certificate update. *Proceedings of the 7th Conference on USENIX Security Symposium*, pp. 17–17, 1998. DOI: 10.1109/49.839932. 45

[108] T. Pedersen. Non-interactive and information-theoretical Secure verifiable secret sharing. *Advances in Cryptology-CRYPTO*, LNCS 576, pp. 129–140, Springer, 1991. DOI: 10.1007/3-540-46766-1_9. 38

[109] C. Papamanthou and R. Tamassia. Time and space efficient algorithms for two-party authenticated data structures. *Information and Communications Security*, LNCS 4861, pp. 1–15, Springer, 2007. DOI: 10.1007/978-3-540-77048-0_1. 45

[110] M. Peter and T. Grance. The NIST definition of cloud computing. *National Institute of Standards and Technology*, 53(6), pp. 50, 2009. DOI: 10.6028/nist.sp.800-145. 2

[111] K. Ren, C. Wang, and Q. Wang. Security Challenges for the Public Cloud. *IEEE Internet Computing*, 16(1), pp. 69–73, 2012. DOI: 10.1109/mic.2012.14. 3

[112] R. Sion. Secure data outsourcing. *Proceedings of the 33rd International Conference on Very Large Data Bases (VLDB)*, pp. 1431–1432, 2007. 45

[113] M. Scott. Unbalancing pairing-based key exchange protocols. *Cryptology*, ePrint Archive/2013/688, 2013. 43

[114] A. Shamir and Y. Tauman. Improved online/offline signature schemes. *Advances in Cryptology-CRYPTO*, LNCS 2139, pp. 355–367, Springer, 2001. DOI: 10.1007/3-540-44647-8_21. 38

[115] C.P. Schnorr. Efficient signature generation for smart cards. *Journal of Cryptology*, 4(3), pp. 239–252, Springer, 1991. DOI: 10.1007/bf00196725. 30, 34

[116] M. Scott, N. Costigan, and W. Abdulwahab. Implementing cryptographic pairings on smartcards. *Cryptographic Hardware and Embedded Systems-CHES*, LNCS 4249, pp. 134–147, Springer, 2006. DOI: 10.1007/11894063_11. 40

[117] S. Subashini and V. Kavitha. A survey on security issues in service delivery models of cloud computing. *Journal of Network and Computer Applications*, 34(1), pp. 1–11, 2011. DOI: 10.1016/j.jnca.2010.07.006.

[118] N.P. Smart and F. Vercauteren. Fully homomorphic encryption with relatively small key and ciphertext sizes. *Public Key Cryptography-PKC*, vol. 6056, pp. 420–443, Springer, 2010. DOI: 10.1007/978-3-642-13013-7_25. 8

[119] H. Shacham and B. Waters. Compact proofs of retrievability. *Asiacrypt*, LNCS 5350, pp. 90–107, Springer, 2008. DOI: 10.1007/978-3-540-89255-7_7. 66

[120] P. Tsang, S. Chow, and S. Smith. Batch pairing delegation. *Advances in Information and Computer Security*, pp. 74–90, Springer, 2007. DOI: 10.1007/978-3-540-75651-4_6.

[121] R. Tamassia and N. Triandopoulos. Certification and authentication of data structures. *Alberto Mendelzon Workshop on Foundations of Data Management*, 2010. 45

[122] H. Tian, F.Zhang, and K. Ren. Secure Bilinear Pairing Outsourcing Made More Efficient and Flexible. *Proceedings of the 10th ACM Symposium on Information, Computer and Communications Security (ASIACCS)*, pp. 417–426, 2015. DOI: 10.1145/2714576.2714615. 42

[123] C. Wang, K. Ren, and J. Wang. Secure and practical outsourcing of linear programming in cloud computing. *Proceedings of the 30th IEEE International Conference on Computer Communications (INFOCOM)*, pp. 820–828, 2011. DOI: 10.1109/infcom.2011.5935305. 19

[124] M. van Dijk, C.Gentry, S. Halevi, and V.Vaikuntanathan. Fully homomorphic encryption over the integers. *Advances in Cryptology-EUROCRYPT*, pp. 24–43, 2010. DOI: 10.1007/978-3-642-13190-5_2. 8

[125] C. Wang, N. Cao, K. Ren, and W. Lou. Enabling Secure and Efficient Ranked Keyword Search over Outsourced Cloud Data. *IEEE Transactions on Parallel Distribution Systems*, 23(8), pp. 1467–1479, 2012. DOI: 10.1109/tpds.2011.282. 3

[126] C. Wang, K. Ren, J. Wang, and Q. Wang. Harnessing the Cloud for Securely Outsourcing Large-scale Systems of Linear Equations. *IEEE Transactions on Parallel Distribution Systems*, 24(6), pp. 1172–1181, 2013. DOI: 10.1109/tpds.2012.206. 19, 25

[127] H. Wang and L.V.S. Lakshmanan. Efficient Secure Query Evaluation over Encrypted xml Databases. *Proceedings of the 32nd International Conference on Very Large Data Bases (VLDB)*, pp. 127–C138, 2006. 45

[128] W. Wu, Y. Mu, W. Susilo, and X. Huang. Server-Aided Verification Signatures: definitions and new constructions. *Provable Security*, LNCS 5324, pp. 141–155, Springer, 2008. DOI: 10.1007/978-3-540-88733-1_10. 34

[129] J. Xu and E.C. Chang. Towards efficient proofs of retrievability in cloud storage. *AsiaCCS*, pp. 79–80, ACM, 2012. DOI: 10.1145/2414456.2414503. 66

[130] A. Yao. Protocols for secure computations. *Proceedings of the IEEE Symposium on Foundations of Computer Science*, pp. 160–164, 1982. DOI: 10.1109/sfcs.1982.38. 8

[131] A. Yao. How to generate and exchange secrets. *Proceedings of the IEEE Symposium on Foundations of Computer Science*, pp. 162–167, 1986. DOI: 10.1109/sfcs.1986.25. 8

[132] R. Yuster and U. Zwick. Fast Sparse Matrix Multiplication. *Annual European Symposium on Algorithms*, LNCS 3221, pp. 604–615, Springer, 2004. DOI: 10.1007/978-3-540-30140-0_54. 27

[133] A.A. Yavuz. Practical immutable signature bouquets (PISB) for authentication and integrity in outsourced databases, *Proceedings of the 27th Annual on Data and Applications Security and Privacy (DBSec)*, pp. 179–194, 2013. DOI: 10.1007/978-3-642-39256-6_12. 45

[134] F. Zhang, X. Ma, and S. Liu. Efficient computation outsourcing for inverting a class of homomorphic functions. *Information Sciences*, 286(1), pp. 19–28, 2014. DOI: 10.1016/j.ins.2014.07.017. 43

Author's Biography

XIAOFENG CHEN

Professor Xiaofeng Chen received his B.S. and M.S. on Mathematics from Northwest University, China, in 1998 and 2000, respectively. He got his Ph.D. degree in Cryptography from Xidian University in 2003. Currently, he works at Xidian University as a professor. His research interests include applied cryptography and cloud computing security. He has published over 100 research papers in refereed international conferences and journals. His work has been cited more than 3,000 times at Google Scholar. He is on the Editorial Board of *Security and Communication Networks* (SCN), *Telecommunication Systems* (TELS), *Computing and Informatics* (CAI), and *International Journal of High Performance Computing and Networking* (IJHPCN), etc. He served as general chair of the 11th ACM Asia Conference on Computer and Communications Security (AsiaCCS 2016) and as program co-chair of the 5th International Conference on Provable Security (ProvSec 2011). He has also served as program committee member in over 30 international conferences. Currently, he is a director of Information Security Center, State Key Laboratory of Integrated Service Networks (ISN), Xidian University.